Front cover: EMU M28219M is seen crossing over to take the down line at Lancaster Green Ayre and then the connecting curve for Lancaster Castle Station on 19th April 1964. (Colour-Rail.com)

Back cover, upper: LNER Class Y7 No 986, BR no. 68089 was purchased from Gateshead and used in 1952 during construction work on Morecambe promenade. On completion of its tasks it was scrapped on site. This locomotive is featured in the Middleton Press album Alnmouth to Berwick, *working on the Chathill and Seahouses line. (N.R.Knight/Manchester Locomotive Society coll.)*

Back cover, lower: Railway Clearing House map, dated 1947. The route of the album is shown with a dotted line.

In memory of

JOHN OAKEY

Published July 2021

ISBN 978 1 910356 58 6

Cover design Deborah Esher
Design Cassandra Morgan

Published by
Middleton Press Ltd
Camelsdale Road
Haslemere
Surrey
GU27 3RJ
Tel: 01730 813169
Email: info@middletonpress.co.uk
www.middletonpress.co.uk

Printed by Mapseeker Digital Ltd, Unit 15, Bridgwater Court, Oldmixon Crescent, Weston Super Mare, North Somerset, BS24 9AY. Telephone +44 (0) 01922 458288 +44 (0) 7947107248

CONTENTS

INDEX

ACKNOWLEDGEMENTS

I am very grateful for the assistance received from many of those mentioned in the credits, and also from G.Croughton, R.Daniels, P.Donnelly, G.Gartside, D.Harris, A.C.Hartless, C.M.Howard, H.Johnston, N.Langridge, Morecambe Library, A.Prykhodko, D.Richardson, D.Salter, P.D.Shannon, M.Stewart, C.Whitaker, and to the late Vic Mitchell.

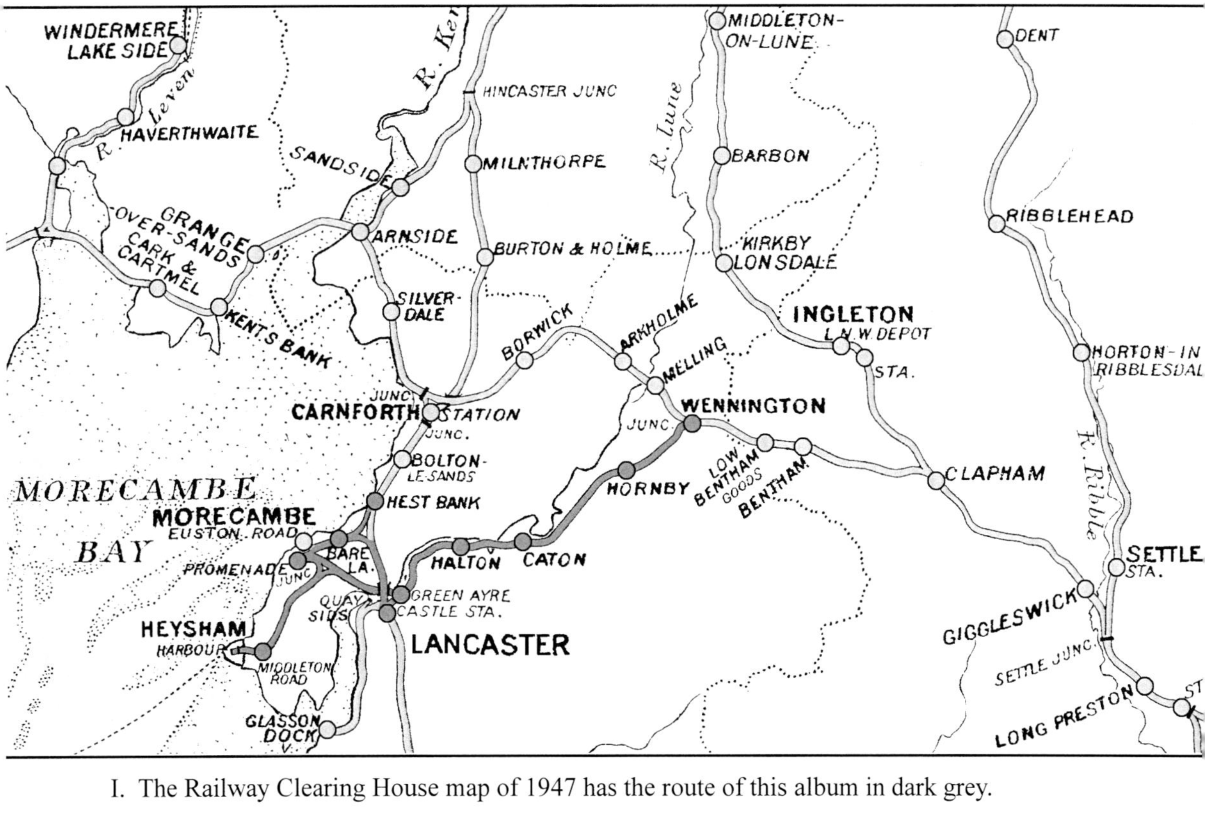

I. The Railway Clearing House map of 1947 has the route of this album in dark grey.

GEOGRAPHICAL SETTING

The small village of Wennington, just inside Lancashire, stands on the River Wenning that joins the Lune about a mile (1.5km) west of Hornby, both of which lie in the Forest of Bowland AONB, as does Caton, which is further to the west. To the north and east, the peaks of the Yorkshire Dales can be seen. After crossing the Lune twice, the line follows it through Halton to the ancient university city of Lancaster, which dates back to Roman and Anglo Saxon times. Famous landmarks include the Castle, Priory Church, Lancaster Cathedral and the Ashton Memorial. Lancaster was once a busy port until superseded by Morecambe and later Heysham (pronounced 'Heeshum'). The geology of the river courses is of a carboniferous millstone grit series of alternating shales, mudstones and sandstones.

Across the River Lune, a coastal development grew up on Morecambe Bay around the railway and harbour close to the village of Poulton-le-Sands that later expanded to absorb the hamlets of Bare and Torrisholme. In 1889, the name Morecambe (from Mwr Cwm, 'Great Bay' of Celtic origin) was adopted officially. The area is bounded to the north by Morecambe Bay, to the west by the Irish Sea, the River Lune Estuary to the south and the West Coast Main Line to the east. There are limestone outcrops in the northwest of the area and around Heysham that give way to soft sediment and superficial deposits in the south over underlying red sandstone. In general, the whole area is relatively flat, but starts to rise to the east as the coastal plain gives way to the Bowland Fells beyond the M6 motorway.

In railway engineering terms, the only obstacle of note on the journey is the River Lune, crossed twice at the Crook O'Lune between Caton and Halton, and again at Lancaster via the Greyhound Bridge.

The maps are to the scale of 25ins to 1 mile, with north at the top, unless otherwise indicated.

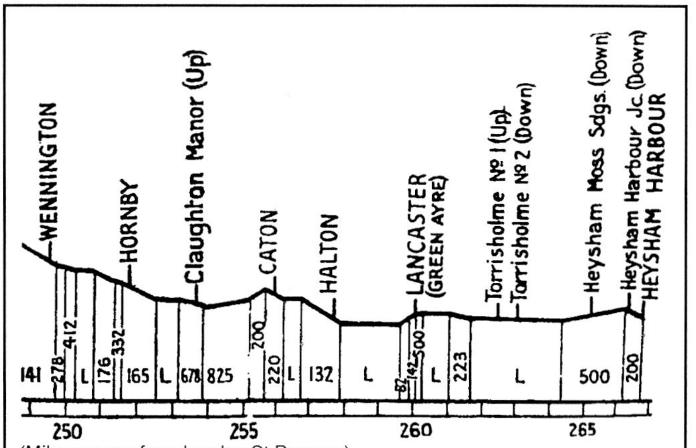

(Mileages are from London St Pancras)

HISTORICAL BACKGROUND

From the early 1800s, Edmund Sharpe, architect, officer of the North Western Railway and Morecambe landowner, had been promoting the idea of building a new harbour at Poulton-le-Sands due to the River Lune silting up at Lancaster and its inability to handle increasingly larger vessels. At the same time, he witnessed growth in visitor numbers to the resort and its lucrative potential. The harbour project was further developed, despite opposition from some Lancaster merchants, with the original intention of linking it to the city via a ship canal, but this proved impracticable mainly on financial grounds. In his 1948 work, *The Rise of Morecambe (1820-62)*, R. G. Armstrong wrote: *'By 1844 Poulton le Sands had become established as a seaside bathing place.'* He continued, *'Here then had emerged a hitherto concealed motive. Not only was Poulton to be made the harbour but it seemed as if Lancaster's prosperity was to be neglected in favour of this 'remunerative part of the project', the further development of Poulton and the financial gain to the promoters of the scheme of whom one (Sharpe) was a landowner at Poulton.'* So, on 16th July 1846, the Morecambe Harbour and Railway Company (MH&R) was duly incorporated and plans were drawn up to connect the harbour to the Lancaster and Carlisle Railway (L&CR) at Hest Bank some 3 miles (5km) to the east. It was intended to bring in minerals from the northeast of England via the South Durham & Lancashire Union Railway and L&CR main lines for export via Morecambe Harbour, but this plan did not materialise until some 18 years later.

Instead a single-track line opened on 12th June 1848 from Poulton-le-Sands to a new station at Lancaster Green Ayre. As all this was happening, the North Western Railway (NWR), known as the 'Little' North Western Railway, was extending the Leeds and Bradford Railway, later absorbed by the Midland Railway (MR) in 1853, west from Skipton in Yorkshire initially towards Clapham and on to Ingleton, which opened on 31st July 1849. Meanwhile, the NWR was constructing the line eastwards from Lancaster Green Ayre to Tatham, which opened on 17th November 1849 and soon after extended further east to Wennington and Bentham, opening on 2nd May 1850; the gap between Bentham and Clapham opened a month later on 1st June 1850. So, by 1850, Morecambe was linked via Wennington and Skipton to the major industrial cities of Leeds and Bradford and the West Riding of Yorkshire. Finally, a short but steep connecting curve from Lancaster Green Ayre to Lancaster Castle station on the L&CR was opened on 18th December 1849.

Long after the original plan was conceived, the branch from Morecambe to the L&CR at Hest Bank finally opened on 8th August 1864 and the projected William Land branch from Morecambe to Hest Bank was abandoned as was the proposed spur from the line to Morecambe pier. The final link to Morecambe came when the London & North Western Railway (LNWR) opened a spur to the L&CR known as the South Curve on 19th May 1888 allowing direct services from Morecambe to Lancaster Castle and beyond to meet ever-increasing holiday traffic. The former LNWR branch to Morecambe is to be covered in detail in the forthcoming *Lancaster to Windermere* album.

Shortly after incorporation of the MH&R, its assets and operations were acquired by the NWR and, from June 1852, the NWR was worked by the Midland Railway, which eventually absorbed both companies on 1st June 1871.

Originally single throughout, the line was doubled in stages: Wennington to Hornby in 1850; Lancaster to Morecambe by 1877 and Hornby to Lancaster by 1889. The spur between Lancaster Green Ayre and Castle remained single-track throughout until taken out of use in 1976.

Morecambe Harbour proved impractical as a port, largely due to its dependency on the tides. In the early 1860s, agreement was reached with the Furness Railway to transfer Northern Ireland passenger services to Piel Harbour, on what is now the Cumbrian coast, reached from Wennington via Carnforth by way of the Furness & Midland Joint Railway (F&MJR) that opened in 1867. In the late 1890s the MR embarked on a plan to open the much larger Heysham Harbour with deep water moorings, enabling it to capitalise on cargo, passenger traffic to Northern Ireland and the Isle of Man and, later, an oil terminal. A branch from the NWR line at Morecambe opened for contractors' traffic on 12th November 1898 and for passenger traffic on 1st September 1904. In April 1975, passenger services to and from Heysham Harbour were withdrawn following cessation of sailings to Belfast, due to the Northern Ireland troubles. However, boat trains from Manchester Victoria and Euston continued to run after the Belfast ferry service was terminated. Both trains were booked to run through to Heysham Harbour but did so on paper only, terminating at Morecambe Promenade as there were no passengers for Heysham. These services could not be withdrawn following the cessation of sailings until proper consultation was undertaken; otherwise, it would be classed as closure of the line for passengers without completing the necessary formalities. Sailings to the Isle of Man had ceased long before, although much later in the 1960s there were weekly excursions. In 1987 there was a full resumption of the ferry service to the island from Heysham along with a daily boat train from Leeds.

In 1906 the MR experimented with electrification of the lines between Morecambe and Heysham with full services to Lancaster commencing in 1908 using a German 6.6kV 25 Hz AC overhead system powered by the MR's own plant at the port. The service was operated from Heysham and Morecambe to Lancaster Green Ayre, with the spur to Lancaster Castle that had opened in 1849. It ran impressively until withdrawal in 1951, after which steam loco-hauled stock was used until 1953, when the lines were re-energised. The service was operated by 'new' electric multiple units until closure to passengers on 3rd January 1966. The experience gained led to BR adopting the 25kV 50Hz AC system across the United Kingdom for main line electrification.

Early on in the life of the line there were various changes as regards passenger stations in and around Morecambe. Initially, Poulton-le-Sands was opened with the commencement of operations in 1848 with unadvertised services to the jetty, most likely mainly goods. The station on Morecambe Harbour opened in 1853 and closed in July 1904, coinciding with the opening of Heysham Harbour station. After a name change and rebuild, Morecambe station closed on 24th March 1907 in favour of the new station nearby, later known as Morecambe Promenade, that opened on the same date. Middleton Road Halt, on the Heysham branch, was opened in July 1904 and closed in June 1905.

The 1923 Grouping witnessed the heyday of the lines to Morecambe and Heysham with regular local services and traffic from the West Riding of Yorkshire. As a popular seaside resort,

Morecambe attracted many visitors carried on excursions from Yorkshire and, as well as local holidaymakers, others came from as far afield as Scotland. Living in the Morecambe area were a number of Yorkshire businessmen and mill owners who found they could commute to Bradford and Leeds by train every day, and so the Residential Express came to be; for some time it even sported a club car. In addition, many people from the West Riding retired to the Lancashire resort; so it is no wonder Morecambe was referred to as Bradford-on-Sea.

Post-1948 saw a decline in rail traffic to the resort, and with the rationalisation of the railways in 1964 it was announced that the former LNWR branch would be retained, even though the ex-Midland route to Lancaster was electrified, more heavily used and shorter in distance than its rival; the retained line did however pass through the busy intermediate station, Bare Lane. The former MR route was closed to passengers on 3rd January 1966 and to freight in 1967. On 3rd June 1967 the last through train ran from Heysham via Lancaster to the West Riding; it was the 15.05 goods from Heysham Moss Sidings to Leeds, Neville Hill. Thereafter, all traffic using the Heysham Harbour branch had to reverse at Morecambe.

The year 1994 saw further rationalisation with closure of Morecambe Promenade station on 7th February and a new station, constructed more or less on the site of the former Morecambe station at the end of Northumberland Street, opened on 29th May 1994. Services now comprise DMU formations from Leeds to Lancaster (reversal) and Morecambe via Wennington and Carnforth on the former F&MJR route, including the daily boat train to Heysham Port station, as well as regular shuttles from Lancaster to and from Morecambe. In 2012, Bare Lane signal box closed and all lines now come under the control of Preston power box. Apart from the passenger services, nuclear flask trains continue to run between Heysham Power Station and Sellafield BNF, and are operated by Direct Rail Services as and when required.

Prior to privatisation, services were provided by North West Regional Railways. This became North Western Trains, won by Great Western Holdings from 2nd March 1997 and was rebranded as First North Western (FNW) in November 1998, which operated services until 11th December 2004. The following day the route became part of the new Northern franchise, won by Serco and Abellio. This expired on 31st March 2016, with Arriva Trains securing the new Northern franchise. This terminated early, on 1st March 2020, when Department for Transport-owned Northern Trains took over. On 21st September 2020, the DfT announced that franchises would be replaced with 'more demanding' Emergency Recovery Management Agreements that would keep the railways running during the Covid 19 pandemic until new arrangements were put in place. In May 2021, the government announced that all services nationally would be operated by Great British Railways (GBR); this would replace Network Rail and also control the contracting of train operations, the setting of fares and timetables and the collection of fare revenue. Train Operating Companies would become subcontractors of GBR on a cost plus basis. Further details were awaited.

ELECTRIFICATION - THE PIONEER LINE

For many enthusiasts, the former Midland route between Lancaster, Morecambe and Heysham is referred to affectionately as the Pioneer Line and for good reason.

'At a Midland board meeting in July 1906, it was decided to electrify the Lancaster-Morecambe-Heysham lines. Sir Ernest Paget, chairman, made it clear at the August half-yearly meeting that he thought electricity to be the motive power of the future. He said that this was partly the reason why this scheme had been introduced - to give the company's officers experience in this field,' (*The Midland Railway North of Leeds*, Peter E. Baughan). Under the sponsorship of Richard Deeley, Chief Mechanical Engineer, also a qualified electrical engineer, of the MR and designer of the 4-4-0 compound locomotive, the line between Morecambe and Heysham was electrified on 13th April 1908. It was extended to Lancaster Green Ayre and Lancaster Castle on 8th June and 14th September 1908, respectively.

Services began using a German 6.6kV 25 Hz AC overhead system powered by the MR's own generating plant at Heysham with overhead wires carried on a mix of steel and wooden gantries. It ran impressively throughout its life and punctuality and reliability compared very favourably with that of the London Underground system. The service was withdrawn 12th February 1951 as the stock was time expired, at which point steam loco-hauled stock ran until 1953. On 17th August

1953 the lines were re-energised and this time the line was converted to 25kV 50Hz AC with power taken from the National Grid.

The original rolling stock consisted of three 60ft driving motor coaches built at the MR's Derby works and six driving trailer coaches, four of which were built at Derby, with the other two converted from steam motor compartment stock. The driving motor coaches had a cab at each end, which allowed trains to run in one or two and three-car formations, while coupled with driving trailers. When the lines were re-energised in 1953, former LNWR fourth-rail DC stock, which had started life on the West London Willesden to Earls Court service, comprising four three-car sets, was transferred to work on the Morecambe and Heysham lines. These units, built by Metropolitan Cammell in 1914, were fitted with various types of rectifiers and pantographs for AC operation. The 'new' EMUs were classified as AM1 stock but were withdrawn before receiving their TOPS Class 301 designation.

After the route was re-energised and with electrification of the WCML in the pipeline, the line between the Carlisle and Ovangle bridges was used by British Railways as a test bed for various experimental cantilever structures from around Europe for Overhead Line Electrification. This included a simulated 'tunnel', ie low level OLE, with all steelwork for the tests provided by BICC Ltd, at its own expense. The aforementioned stretch of track through Scale Hall station became known as the 'Golden Mile' and it was the successful testing of various rolling stock equipment and OLE that led to the decision to choose 25 kV AC overhead electrification as standard across the UK. However, electrification of the northern section of the WCML on 6th May 1974 came too late to link up with the erstwhile Morecambe and Heysham electrified branches.

Given that the former Midland route from Lancaster to Morecambe and Heysham was the first single-phase electric railway in the country that ran successfully for over half a century, together with its contribution later to UK-wide main line and high-speed railways electrification, the title 'Pioneer Line' is most appropriate.

PASSENGER SERVICES

Before the railway came to Morecambe it was already a popular resort. Passenger numbers were high from the outset, with regular fast services from Leeds and Bradford and the intermediate towns en route of Keighley and Skipton, as well as through services from London. Stopping services along the route also swelled passenger numbers. This popularity led the LNWR to create its own branch from Lancaster and terminus at Morecambe Euston Road. Passenger numbers were further swelled by the introduction of the electric suburban network linking Lancaster with Morecambe and Heysham with a regular and punctual service that lasted nearly 60 years, until closure of the former Midland route in early 1966. The resort came into its own during the summer months when on a Saturday many excursions and specials descended on the town from far and wide, with space for stabling trains at a premium. In post-World War II years, visitor numbers to the resort dwindled, particularly after closure of the former Midland route from Wennington in the 1960s to a point where, in the 1980s, Morecambe Promenade station was larger than required and was closed in 1994 in the next phase of rationalisation.

In the 1880-90s rail passengers arrived at Morecambe jetty from Yorkshire via Lancaster for sailings to Barrow, Fleetwood, Belfast and the Isle of Man, although passenger vessels visiting both Morecambe and Barrow started to reduce in numbers after the opening of the new harbour at Heysham in 1904. However, the new facility was host to boat trains from London and Manchester Victoria serving passengers to Belfast and the Isle of Man, and there is still a daily boat train to Heysham albeit a DMU shuttle from Lancaster for sailings to Douglas.

Post-1994 a regular DMU service to Morecambe/Heysham operates from Leeds via the former F&MJR line from Wennington to Carnforth, reversing at Lancaster for the coast augmented by regular shuttles from Lancaster. At the time of publishing this album, the UK was emerging from the Covid-19 pandemic, during which time passenger numbers fell considerably on the Morecambe route, to the extent that services to Yorkshire were terminated at Skipton. The new timetable effective from 16th May 2021, coinciding with the government's easing of pandemic restrictions, shows a return of through trains from Leeds to Morecambe and Heysham reversing at Lancaster, along with the regular shuttle service between the city and the resort.

October 1912

MORECAMBE, HEYSHAM, LAKE DISTRICT, AND THE FURNESS LINE.

WEEKDAYS—Continued.

London (St. Pancras) dep.	9 30	..	9 30	*11 30*	11 30	..	*12 0*	*12 0*	*12 0*	12 0	1 30	..	1 30	—	3※30	..	..	6 0	6 0
Leicester „	11 25	....	11 25	*1 28*	1 28	....	*2 5*	*2 5*	*2 5*	2 5	3 18	....	3 18	....	5※ 0	....	....	6L35	6 35
Nottingham „	11 28	..	11 28	*12※55*	12※55	..	*2 43*	*2 43*	*2 43*	2 43	2 47	..	2 47	..	5※50	..	..	7L22	7 22
Bristol (Temple Mead) dep.	8※ 0	....	8※ 0	*10 40*	10※40	*Will not run on Bank Holidays and day following.*	*Saturdays excepted.*	*Saturdays excepted.*	*Saturdays excepted.*	....	12 20	....	12 20	....	2※17	....	....	4 52	4 52
Bournemouth „	..	..	..	*8 37*	8※37					..	9 40	..	9 40	..	..	..	..	2 5	2 5
Bath „	7※48	....	7※48	*10 32*	10※32					....	11 57	....	11 57	....	1※50	....	....	4 35	4 35
Gloucester „	9※ 0	..	9※ 0	*11 32*	11※32					..	12 50	..	12 50	..	3※10	..	..	5 55	5 55
Southampton (Docks) „	....	....	....	*7 25*	7※25					....	10 5	....	10 5	....	....	....	....	1 45	1 45
Cheltenham „	9※12	..	9※12	*11 45*	11※45					..	1 20	..	1 20	..	3※24	..	..	6 7	6 7
Birmingham „	10 25	....	10 25	*12 48*	12※48					....	2 25	....	2 25	....	4 28	....	....	7 10	7 10
Derby „	11 30	..	11 30	*1 45*	1※45		*2 5*	*2 5*	*2 5*	2 5	3 28	..	3 28	..	5 30	..	..	8 10	8 10
Buxton (via Hope) „	9 15	....	9 15	*11 10*	11 10		*1 35*	*1 35*	*1 35*	1 35	1 35	....	1 35	....	4 52	....	....	5 35	5 35
Sheffield „	12 3	..	12 3	*1 55*	1 55		*3 52*	*3 52*	*3 52*	3 52	4 40	..	4 40	..	6 50	..	..	9 14	9 14
N. E. Rly. Newcastle dep.	10 28	....	10 28	*12 30*	12 30		....	....	....	....	2 40	....	2 40	....	5 4	....	....	....	7 8
Stockton „	11 16	..	11 16	*12 42*	12 42		..	..	..	..	2 3	..	2 3	..	5 36	..	..	3 14	7 41
Scarboro' „	10 35	....	10 35	*1 17*	1 17		*2 40*	*2 40*	*2 40*	2 40	....	....	....	....	5 55	....	....	....	8 0
York „	12 20	..	12 20	*2 35*	2 35		*3 45*	*3 45*	*3 45*	3 45	4 30	—	4 30	..	7 0	..	..	8 10	9 35
Hull „	10u15	....	10u15	*2 5*	2 5		*2 47*	*2 47*	*2 47*	2 47	4 3	....	4 3	....	5 12	....	....	5 55	8 40
Harrogate „	12 27	..	12 27	*2 28*	2 28		..	..	..	..	4 41	..	4 41	..	6 49	..	..	8 41	9 56
Leeds dep.	1 52	....	1 52	*3 38*	3 38		*4 58*	*4 58*	*4 58*	4 58	5 35	....	5 40	....	7 55	....	....	10 5	10 55
Bradford „	1 52	..	1 52	*3 42*	3 42		*5 10*	*5 10*	*5 10*	5 10	5J10	..	5 28	..	7 35	..	..	9R35	10 47
Halifax, G.N. (via K'ley) „	1 13	....	1 13	*3 20*	3 20		*4 40*	*4 40*	*4 40*	4 40	4J40	....	4 40	....	7 28	....	....	8R53	9 35
Keighley „	2 28	..	2 28	*4 14*	4 14		*5 30*	*5 30*	*5 30*	5 30	5J30	..	6 17	..	8 30	..	..	10R 5	11 20
Ilkley „	2 0	....	2 0	*2 0*	2 0		*4 48*	*4 48*	*4 48*	4 48	4 48	....	6D 3	....	7 5	....	....	8R25	8 25
Grassington & Threshfield „	12V15	..	12V15	*3 50*	3 50		..	..	..	..	..	..	5 18	..	6T38	..	..	6a38	6b38
Skipton „	2 45	....	2 51	*4 30*	4 30		*5 25*	*5 25*	*5 25*	5 25	5 25	....	6 42	....	8 52	....	....	10R40	11 35
Manchester (Victoria) dep.	12 30	..	12 30	*2 25*	2 25		*3 28*	*3 28*	*3 28*	—	4 35	..	4 35	..	..	..	..	8R35	8 35
Bolton (Trinity Street) „	12 49	..	12 49	*2 44*	2 44		*2 50*	*2 50*	*2 50*	....	4 54	....	4 54	....	....	....	....	8R55	8 55
Darwen „	1 12	..	1 12	*3 6*	3 6		*4 5*	*4 5*	*4 5*	..	5 18	..	5 18	..	..	..	..	8R46	8 46
Liverpool (Exchange) „	12 35	....	12 35	*2 20*	2 20		....	....	....	....	4 35	....	4 35	....	....	....	....	6R45	6 45
Accrington „	1 7	..	1 7	*2 56*	2 56		*3 58*	*3 58*	*3 58*	3 58	5 7	..	5 7	..	..	..	..	9R 3	9 3
Blackburn „	1 31	....	1 31	*3 28*	3 28		*4 25*	*4 25*	*4 25*	4 25	5 32	....	5 40	....	....	....	....	9R33	9 33
Clitheroe „	1 49	..	1 49	*3 56*	3 56	..	*4 51*	*4 51*	*4 51*	4 51	5 50	..	6 8	..	..	..	..	9R59	9 59
Hellifield arr.	2 8	....	2 8	*4 33*	4 32	....	*5 22*	*5 22*	*5 22*	5 22	6 10	....	6 40	....	....	....	....	10R27	10 27
Edinburgh dep.	9 30	..	9 30	*10 30*	10 30		..	..	..	..	..	..	..	..	2 15			6R 0	6 0
Glasgow „	9 20	....	9 20	*11 0*	11 0		*1 30*	*1 30*	*1 30*	1 30	1 30	....	1 30	....	....			5R30	5 30

HELLIFIELD dep.	3 3	..	3 15	*4 55*	4 58	5 4	*Saturdays excepted.*	*6 0*	*6 3*	*6 0*	6 3	6 30	..	7 6	..	9 24	*Saturdays excepted.*	*Saturdays only.*	G Through Carriages London & Bristol to Heysham.	11 52
Long Preston	....	....	3 18			5 7		*Saturdays excepted.*	*6 6*	....	6 6	....	....	7 9	....	9 27				....
Giggleswick	X	..	3 26		E	5 15			*6 13*	*Saturdays excepted.*	6 14	H	..	7 17	..	9 35				..
Clapham	....	....	3 37		E	5 27			....		6 25	H	....	7 28	....	9 47				....
Ingleton arr.	..	..	..	*Fridays and Saturdays only.* Will not run until May 9th.	E ..	5 43			*Saturdays excepted.*		7p27	..	..	8 20	..	..				..
Ingleton dep.	....	....	3 5		3 5	3 5					....	....	....	6 50	....	7p35		....		....
Bentham	..	..	3 44		E	5 36					6 32	N	..	7 35	..	9 56		10 20		..
Wennington arr.	....	....	3 49		5 29	5 41					....	....	....	7 40	....	....		10 25		....
Wennington (for M'cambe) dep.	..	..	3 50		..	5 43						..	..	7 46	..	..		10 26		..
Hornby	....	....	3 56		....	5 49		F			F	....	....	7 52	....	....	....	10 32		....
Caton	..	..	4 3		..	5 56	*6 15*	M			M	..	..	7 59	..	..	10 15	10 39		..
Halton	....	....	4 7		....	6 0	*6 20*	....			6 53	....	....	8 3	....	....	10 19	10 43		....
Lancaster (Green Ayre) arr.	..	..	4 12		..	6 5	*6 25*	*6 36*			6 58	..	..	8 8	..	10 13	10 24	10 48		..
Lancaster (Castle) „	....	....	4 25		....	....	....	....		....	....	....	....	....	....	....	....	....		....
MORECAMBE „	..	..	4 22		..	6 15	..	*6 44*		*6 44*	7 7	—	..	8 18	..	10 25	*11 2*	*11 2*		..
Heysham arr.	....	....	4 48		....	6 38	....	....	....	....	7 40	....	....	8 38	....	10 45	....	....	11 47	....
Heysham dep.	..	..	..		..	..	..	Will not run after April 30th. : *Will not run on Bank Holidays.*	Will not run after April 30th. *Will not run on Bank Holidays.*	Will not run until May 1st. *Will not run on Bank Holidays.*	..	..	..	9 0	..	12 0	..	..	12 0	..
Belfast (via Heysham) arr.	....	....	....		....	....	....				Will not run until May 1st. *Will not run on Bank Holidays.*	....	....	....	....	6 15	....	....	6 15	....
Dublin („) „	..	..	..		..	..	..					..	..	7 0	..	..	..	..	....	..
Wennington (for C'forth) dep.	....	....	....		5 31	....	....					....	....	7 48	....	....	....	....		....
Melling	..	..	..		5 35	..	..					..	..	7 47	..	..	..	..	Belfast Boat Corridor Express. 1st and 3rd Class Restaurant Cars London to Heysham.	..
Arkholme (for K. Lonsdale)	y	....	....	m	5 39	....	....					K	....	7 52	....	....	....	....		....
Borwick	..	..	..	..	5 47	..	..					..	..	..	..	..	..	..		....
CARNFORTH arr.	3 45	....	....	*5 40*	5 53	....	....					7 12	....	8 2	....	....	....	....		12 35
Furness Railway. Carnforth dep.	4 0	....	....	....	6 10	....	....					7 23	....	8 15	....	....	....	....		4 25
Silverdale arr.	4 14	..	..	*5 48*	6 19	..	..					..	..	8 24	..	..	..	..		7 9
Arnside „	4 21	....	....	*5 54*	6 26	....	....					....	....	8 31	....	....	....	....		7 16
Grange „	4 14	..	..	*6 1*	6 33	..	..					SC	..	8 38	..	..	..	..		7 23
Kendal „	5 10	....	....	..	7 25	....	....					....	....	....	....	....	....	....		8U55
Cark & Cartmel „	4 41	..	..	*6A14*	6 46	..	..					..	..	8 51	..	..	..	..		7 36
Ulverston „	4 30	....	....	*6 27*	6 59	....	....					7 49	....	9 4	....	....	....	....		4 54
Lake Side (Windermere) „	5 25	..	..	*6 45*	7 30	..	..					..	..	..	..	..	..	..		9U45
Bowness (by Steamer) „	6 5	....	....	*7 30*	....	....	....					....	....	....	....	....	....	....		10U25
Ambleside (by Steamer) „	6 40	..	..	*8 5*	..	..	..	..	..	..	..	..	..	..	..	..	..	..		11U 0
Grasmere (by Coach) „	....	....	....	*8 50*	....	....	....					....	....	....	....	....	....	....		11U50
Dalton „	5 10	..	..	*6 41*	7 15	..	..					7A59	..	9 20	..	..	..	..		5 8
Furness Abbey „	4A46	....	....	*6 46*	7 20	....	....					8A 4	....	9 25	....	....	....	....		8 10
Barrow (Ramsden Dk.) „	..	..	..	..	..	..	..					8B25	..	..	..	..	..	..		..
Barrow (Central) „	4 52	....	....	*6 53*	7 30	....	....					8 10	....	9 35	....	....	....	....		5 17
Belfast (via Barrow) „	....	..	..	—	..	..	..					5P30	..	....	....	....	....	....		....
Foxfield „	5A16	....	....	....	....	....	....					8 41	....	*11Q26*	....	....	....	....		5 41
Coniston Lake „	6 45	..	..	..	..	..	..					..	..	..	..	..	..	..		9 25
Millom „	5 25	....	....	....	....	....	....					8 56	....	*11Q38*	....	....	....	....		5 53
Ravenglass (for Eskdale) „	5 48	..	..	..	..	..	..					9 23	..	..	..	..	..	..		9 30
Seascale „	5 58	....	....	....	....	....	....					9 33	....	....	....	....	....	....		6 20
St. Bees „	6 17	..	..	..	..	..	..					9 55	..	..	..	..	..	..		6 37
Whitehaven „	6 30	....	....	....	....	....	....					10 8	....	....	....	....	....	....		6 50
Workington „	7 8	..	..	*10t 7*	..	..	..					10 35	..	..	..	..	..	..		8 18
L. & N. W. Carnforth dep.	3 54	..	..	*6 2*	6 2	..	..					7 20	..	8 10	..	..	..	..		3 49
Kendal arr.	4 30	....	....	*6 28*	6 28	....	....					7 45	....	8 47	....	....	....	....		4 29
Windermere „	4 57	..	..	*6 57*	6 57	..	..	..	..	..	..	8 12	—	9 14	..	..	..	—	..	4 50
Penrith „	5 13	....	....	*7 31*	7 31	....	....	....	....	....	....	....	....	....	....	....	....	....	....	4 55
Keswick „	6 28	..	..	*9 10*	9 10	..	..	..	..	..	..	..	..	..	..	..	..	..	..	8 20
Cockermouth „	6 58	....	....	*9 40*	9 40	....	....	....	....	....	....	....	....	....	....	....	....	....	....	8 48

A Sets down from Stations beyond Carnforth.
B Tuesdays, Thursdays, and Saturdays only.
D 5.27 p.m. on Saturdays until March 31st.
E Takes up for Melling and beyond.
F Sets down from Keighley and beyond.
G Takes up Passengers for Ireland.
H Takes up Passengers for Stations beyond Carnforth.
J Bank Holidays excepted. Bradford 4.50, Halifax 3.20, and Keighley 5.13 p.m. on Saturdays until April 30th.
K Sets down Passengers from Bradford, Leeds, and beyond, Carlisle and beyond, also from Manchester and Liverpool.
L Passengers for Belfast leave Leicester 7.35 and Nottingham 7.42.
M Sets down Passengers from Bradford.
N Stops on Tuesdays and Thursdays to set down from Leeds and Bradford.
P Wednesday, Friday, and Sunday mornings **only**.
Q Saturdays only.
R These times apply to Passengers for Ireland only.

T 7.55 p.m. during May and June.
U Sundays excepted.
V 1.48 p.m. on Saturdays during June.
X Takes up for Carnforth and beyond.
a This time applies to Passengers for Ireland only. Will leave at 7.55 p.m. during May and June (9.10 on Saturdays in June).
b 7.55 p.m. during May and June (9.10 p.m. on Saturdays in June).
m Sets down from Bradford and Leeds and beyond, also from Manchester and Liverpool.
p Tuesdays and Saturdays only, and will not apply until May 10th.
t Via Penrith. **u** 11.0 a.m. on Tuesdays.
y Sets down from Bradford, Leeds, and beyond, the L. & Y. Line, via Hellifield, also from Stations on the Settle and Carlisle Line.
※ Bank Holidays excepted.

SC Sets down Passengers by Slip Carriage at 7.36 p.m.

For Sunday Train Service, see page 93.

June 1965

London, Manchester, Leeds to Belfast via Heysham

(Subject to alteration during Christmas 1965 and Easter 1966 periods)

		Monday to Friday nights								Saturday nights						Sunday nights 11 July to 15 August						
		B FX	A FX	FO		The Ulster Express								The Ulster Express				The Ulster Express				
LONDON EUSTON	d					17 45								18 45				16 10				
BIRMINGHAM NEW STREET	d	*18 00*	18 25	18 25						18 25								*17 40*				
CREWE	d	20 02	20 02	20 02		20u39				20 02				21 39				19 27				
MANCHESTER VICTORIA	d						20 55				21 05									21 05		
BOLTON TRINITY STREET	d						21 16				21 26									21 28		
CHORLEY	d						21 37				21 46									21 49		
PRESTON	d	21 11	21 11	21 j11		21 45	22 02			21k11	22 06			22 45						22 13		
LEEDS CITY	d							21 32					21 32								21 48	
BRADFORD FORSTER SQUARE	d							*21 10*					*21 10*								*21 35*	
KEIGHLEY	d							21 58					21 58								22 14	
SKIPTON	d							22 13					22 13								22 30	
HEYSHAM	a	21 57	21 57	22 20		22 36	22 53	23 20		22 20	23 00		23 20	23 33				22 00		23 10	23 35	
HEYSHAM SHIP	d	23 40								00 40						23 40						
BELFAST DONEGALL QUAY SHIP	a	06 45								07 45						06 45						

June 1965

Lancaster to Morecambe and Heysham

Miles	Miles	Miles				2	2	A SX	2	2			2	A SX	2			2	B SO	SX 2	SO 2	C SX	SO	A SX
0	0	0	LANCASTER CASTLE	d		06 33	07 55	08 10		08 25			08 55	09 09	09 25		09 50	09 55		10 25	10 25			10 30
½	½	—	LANCASTER GREEN AYRE	d		06 38	07 59			08 29		08 40	08 59		09 29			09 59	10 19	10 29	10 29	10 33	10 33	
1¼	1¼	—	SCALE HALL	d			08 02			08 32			09 02		09 32			10 02		10 32	10 32			
—	—	2½	BARE LANE	d				08 16						09 15			09 56							10 36
—	4	4¼	MORECAMBE PROMENADE	a		06 44	08 07	08 21		08 37		08 48	09 07	09 20	09 37		10 01	10 07	10 27	10 37	10 37	10 41	10 41	10 42
				d		06 50			08 30						09 45					10 41	10 41			
7½	8½	—	HEYSHAM	a		07 02			08 39						09 54					10 50	10 52			

			2	A SX	B SO	2	D SO	2	B	A SX	2	2	SO	SO	SX	2	SO 2	SX 2	2	SO	SX 2	2		
LANCASTER CASTLE	d		10 55			11 25				11 47	11 55	12 25				12 55			13 25			13 55		
LANCASTER GREEN AYRE	d		10 59	10 59		11 29	11 33				11 59	12 29	12 42	12 51	12 53	12 59			13 29	13 48	13 57	13 59		
SCALE HALL	d		11 02			11 32					12 02	12 32				13 02			13 32		13 59	14 02		
BARE LANE	d				11 10				11 44	11 53														
MORECAMBE PROMENADE	a		11 07	11 07	11 15	11 37	11 41		11 54	11 58	12 07	12 37	12 50	12 59	13 00	13 07			13 37	13 56	14 05	14 07		
	d							11 50									13 12	13 23				14 13		
HEYSHAM	a							12 01									13 23	13 34				14 22		

				SO	2	2		2	2				2	C	2		A SX	2			2			E SO
LANCASTER CASTLE	d				14 25	14 55		15 25	15 55			16 11	16 25	16 43	16 55		17 05				17 25			
LANCASTER GREEN AYRE	d			14 16	14 29	14 59		15 29	15 59	16 06			16 29		16 59					17 27	17 29			
SCALE HALL	d				14 32	15 02		15 32	16 02				16 32		17 02						17 32			
BARE LANE	d											16 17		16 50			17 11							17 52
MORECAMBE PROMENADE	a			14 24	14 37	15 07		15 37	16 07	16 14		16 22	16 37	16 54	17 07		17 16			17 34	17 37			17 57
	d					15 15							16 45					17 20						
HEYSHAM	a					15 24							16 54					17 29						

			C	2	B SO	A SX	A SX		2	SX			B SO		2		B		2	2	2			
LANCASTER CASTLE	d		17 52	17 55	17 58	18 10			18 25					18 46	18 55		19 20		19 25		19 55			
LANCASTER GREEN AYRE	d			17 59					18 29	18 42					18 59	19 09			19 29		19 59	20 09		
SCALE HALL	d			18 02					18 32						19 02				19 32		20 02			
BARE LANE	d		17 58		18 05	18 16	18 20						18 48	18 52			19 26							
MORECAMBE PROMENADE	a		18 03	18 07	18 10	18 21	18 25		18 37	18 50			18 53	18 57	19 07	19 17	19 31		19 37		20 07	20 17		
	d																			19 55				
HEYSHAM	a																			20 04				

		2	2	2	2		F	2		G FSO	SX 2	SX 2	SO 2	SX	SO	SO	SX 2	SO 2			H SO	2		
LANCASTER CASTLE	d	20 25		20 55	21 25			21 55				22 25	22 25	22 28	22 35		22 55	22 55				23 25		
LANCASTER GREEN AYRE	d	20 29		20 59	21 29			21 59				22 29	22 29			22 50	22 59	22 59	23 06			23 29		
SCALE HALL	d	20 32		21 02	21 32			22 02				22 32	22 32					23 02						
BARE LANE	d																							
MORECAMBE PROMENADE	a	20 37		21 07	21 37			22 07				22 37	22 37	22 38	22 45	22 58	23 07	23 07				23 36		
	d		20 50				21 47			22 10	22 25		22 40	22 43	22 50						23 16			
HEYSHAM	a		20 59				21 57			22 20	22 34		22 49	22 53	23 00				23 20		23 26			

Heavy figures denote through carriages
For general notes see page 4

A Until 3 September
B Until 4 September
C From 6 September
D 24 July to 4 September
E 26 June to 21 August
F Not on Fridays and Saturdays after 4 September
G From 10 September
H 3 July to 4 September

1. Wennington to Lancaster

WENNINGTON

II. This 1913 map of the station shows all the paraphernalia of a busy junction, including sidings, a bay platform and turntable for what was, and still is, a small village. Today, the line between Settle Junction and Carnforth, just over 24 miles, is the longest absolute block section in the UK, and Wennington is some 15 miles into it. To the west of the station is the site of the accident referred to in caption 1. A little to the west of Wennington was the short-lived Wray Station; it opened in November 1949 and closed some six months later.

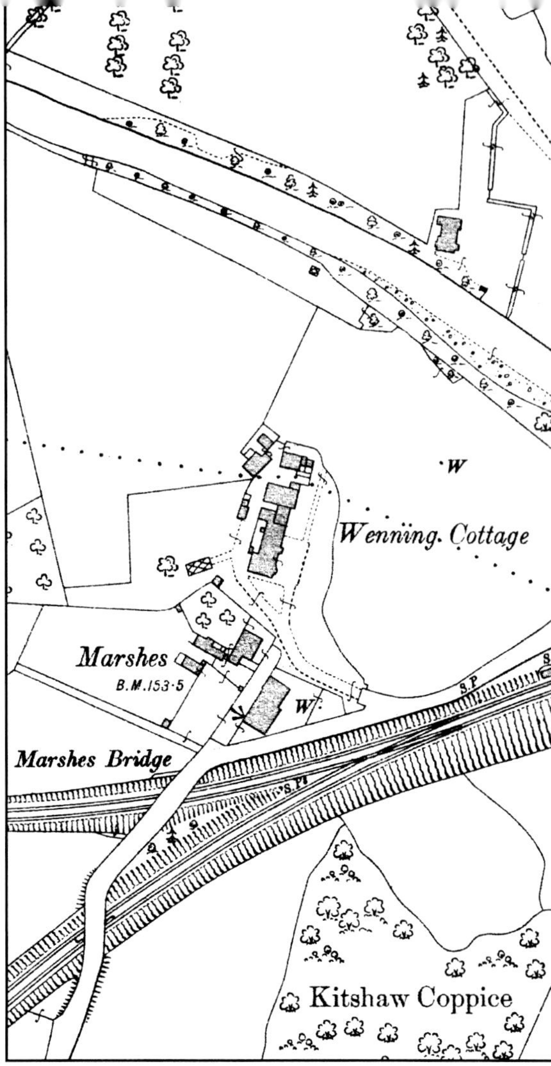

➜ 1. The original line to Lancaster and Wennington was served by a temporary station at Tatham Bridge (17th November 1849 to 1st May 1850), less than a mile to the west of the current station; at this time the line did not extend east towards Bentham. The current Wennington station was opened on 2nd May 1850, which coincided with the doubling of the line from Hornby to Wennington and further east to Hellifield. This undated photograph shows Wennington station looking east with a loco shunting in the goods yard. On the afternoon of 11th August 1880 the 12.15pm express from Leeds to Lancaster and Morecambe became derailed at the junction with the F&MJR. The train somehow managed to travel another 200yds west and the coaches hit the abutment of the overbridge destroying a number of them. According to reports, *'Seven passengers are returned as having been killed on the spot and one has since died of the injuries which he received, and 23 other passengers were also injured, some of them most severely'*. (Robert Humm coll.)

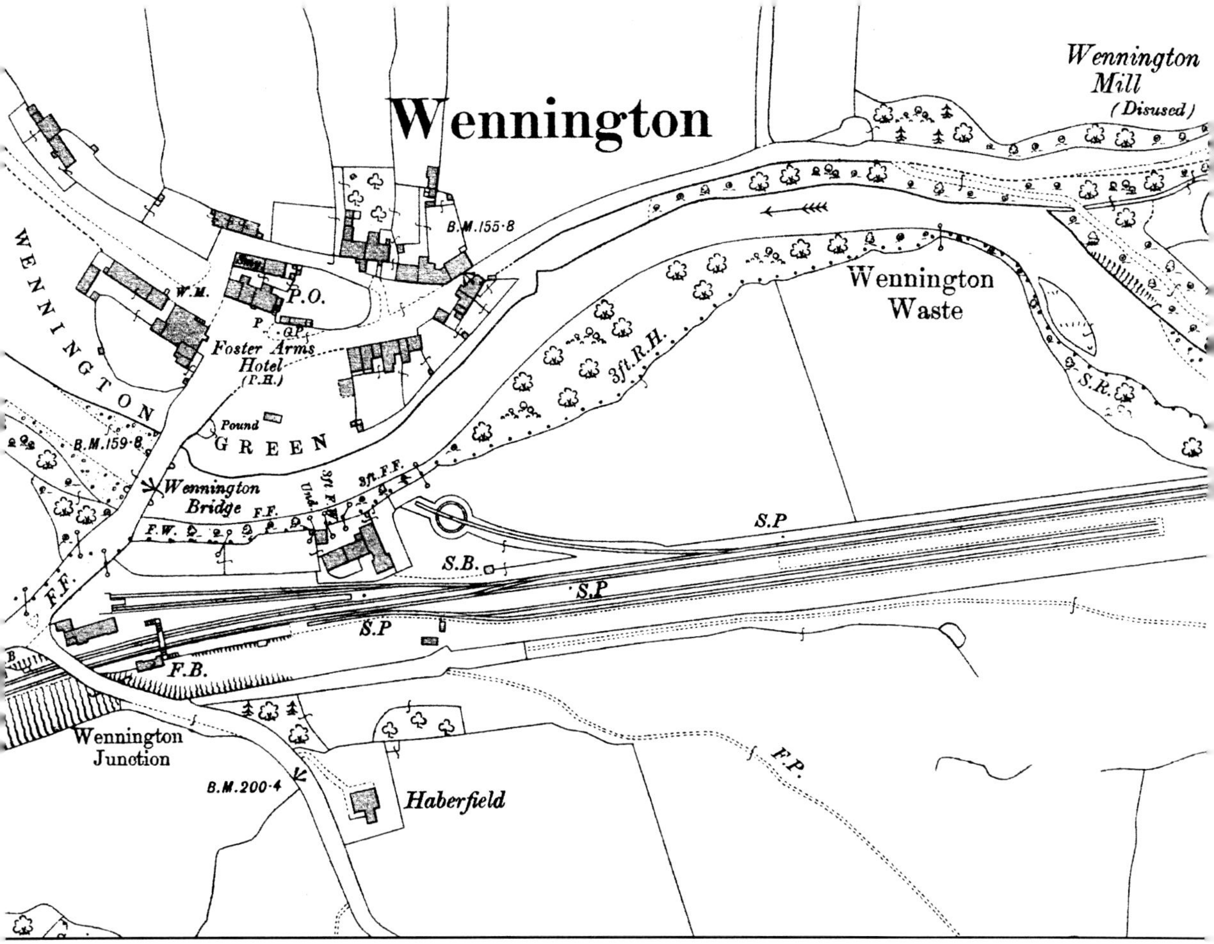

2. In this undated shot looking west, LMS 4P Compound 4-4-0 no. 41108 enters the up platform. The coaches in the bay platform will be attached to the through Leeds train, after its station stop, by drawing forward and reversing into the bay under the control of a covered ground frame to the east of the station. (Cumbria Railway Association, 'CRA')

3. Leeds Holbeck ex-LMS Stanier 'Jubilee' 5P (BR 6P) 4-6-0 no. 44573 *Newfoundland* passes Wennington Junction signal box on 12th September 1964 with the 2.46pm Morecambe–Leeds train. Standing on the down Lancaster line is Fowler class 4MT 2-6-4T no. 42359, which had arrived at Wennington with the Carnforth portion. It is stood on the down Lancaster line awaiting the arrival of a Leeds to Carnforth train that will detach a Morecambe portion in Wennington station to be worked forward by the Fowler tank. (Noel Machell)

➔ 4. In this undated shot, Stanier ex-LMS 4MT 2-6-4T no. 42571 couples up to stock waiting in the down platform with a Morecambe-bound train. As in the previous photo, this locomotive would have stood on the Lancaster down line awaiting departure of the Carnforth portion and then reversed into Wennington to work the Morecambe portion forward. (CRA)

↓ 5. Ex-LMS Stanier 5MT 'Black 5' 4-6-0 no. 44889 heads the Saturdays only 12.43 Bradford to Morecambe 'Residential Express' through Wennington station on 17th July 1965. The 2-6-4T in the background is awaiting its next turn of duty after arriving at Wennington with the Carnforth portion of a previous Morecambe to Leeds train. (Noel Machell)

6. Looking east on 18th February 1967 from the station footbridge, Black 5 no. 44662 is being re-railed after coming off the tracks at the east end of the station. The loco was withdrawn in October of that year. (CRA)

➔ 7. BR Class 142 Pacer DMU Rail Bus no. 142089 pauses in the westbound platform with a Leeds to Lancaster working on 8th September 1989. It is reported that no passengers joined or alighted from the train that day. On 3rd January 1966 the former Midland line to Lancaster was closed to passenger services and, thereafter the city was reached via Carnforth with trains generally reversing at Lancaster for onward trips to Morecambe and Heysham. Note that all station buildings had been demolished by then and passenger shelters erected on each platform. Wennington signal box opened on 31st May 1890 and, in April 2006, the box was closed and, within a short time, was dismantled for use on the Poulton & Wyre Railway. (Noel Machell)

WEST OF WENNINGTON

Hindburn Bridge

8. BR Sulzer Type 2 Class 25 D5178, working the 3.14pm from Leeds City to Morecambe Promenade on 3rd June 1963, crosses the Hindburn Bridge between Wennington and Hornby, which was later washed away in the tragic floods in the summer of 1967. Freight had ceased by then, but it is very unlikely its demise would have had any effect on saving the line, as Lancaster City Council had already earmarked the Greyhound Bridge in the city as a second road river crossing to relieve traffic congestion on Skerton Bridge. (Noel Machell)

HORNBY

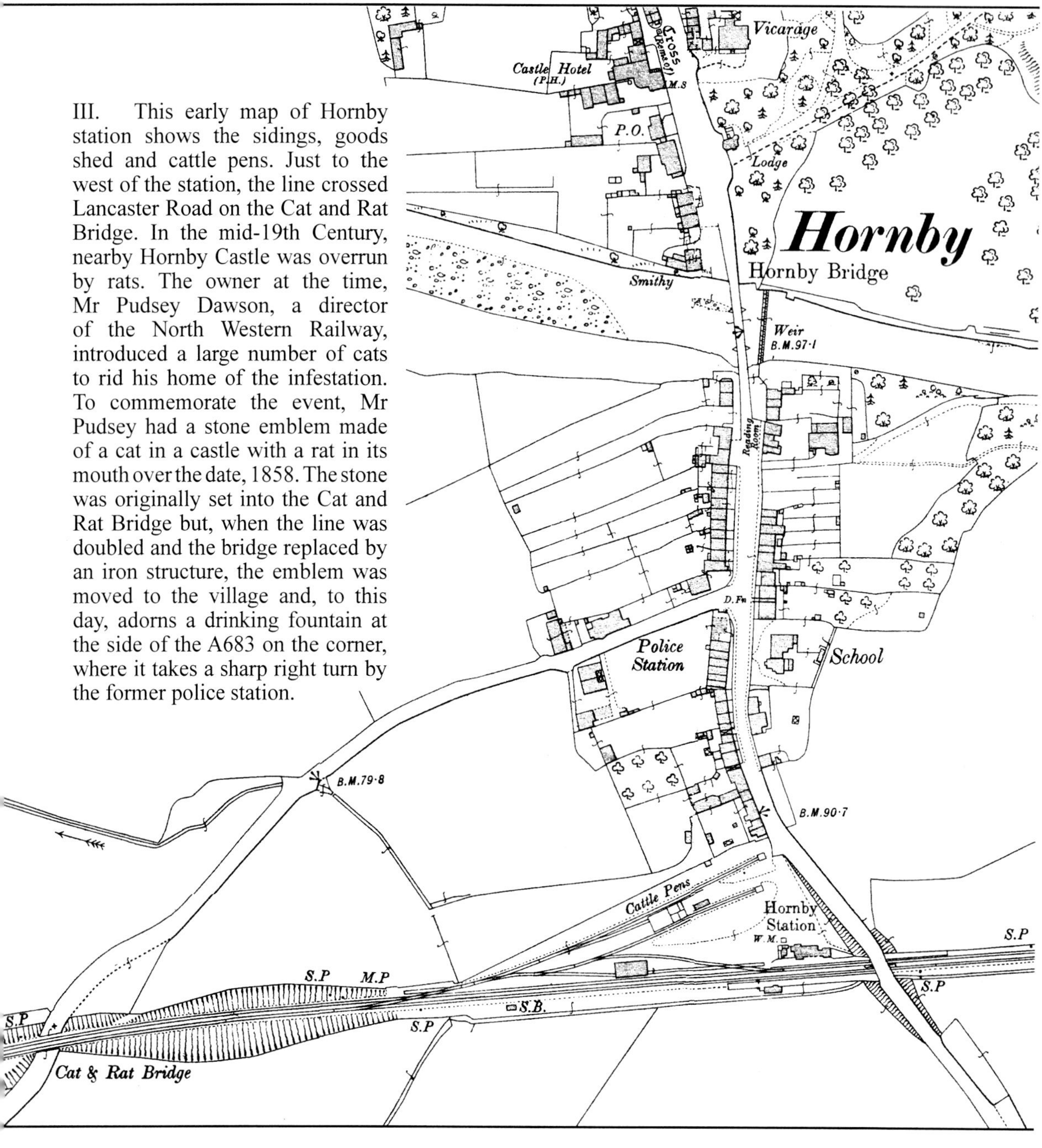

III. This early map of Hornby station shows the sidings, goods shed and cattle pens. Just to the west of the station, the line crossed Lancaster Road on the Cat and Rat Bridge. In the mid-19th Century, nearby Hornby Castle was overrun by rats. The owner at the time, Mr Pudsey Dawson, a director of the North Western Railway, introduced a large number of cats to rid his home of the infestation. To commemorate the event, Mr Pudsey had a stone emblem made of a cat in a castle with a rat in its mouth over the date, 1858. The stone was originally set into the Cat and Rat Bridge but, when the line was doubled and the bridge replaced by an iron structure, the emblem was moved to the village and, to this day, adorns a drinking fountain at the side of the A683 on the corner, where it takes a sharp right turn by the former police station.

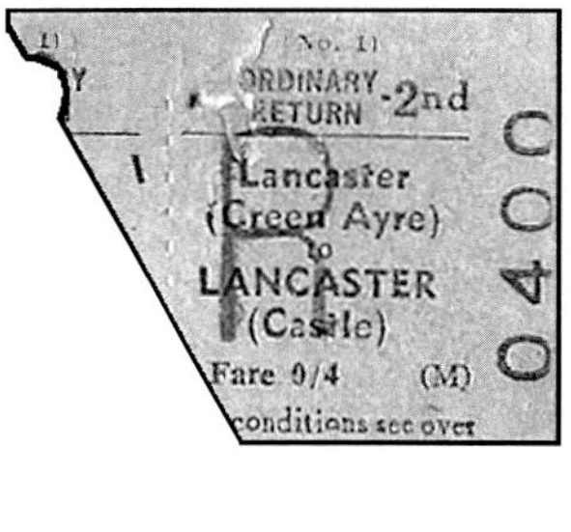

9. Hornby station opened on 17th November 1849 and became Hornby for Kirkby Lonsdale (some 8 miles away) on 1st April 1851. It reverted to Hornby on 1st January 1863. Of interest is the very tall MR signal at the end of the platform next to the overbridge.
(Roy F. Burrows Midland Collection Trust/Kidderminster Railway Museum, 'KRM')

10. This 1958 shot looking west from the overbridge shows ex-LMS Fowler 0-6-0 4F no. 44431 heading east. This photo gives a general view of the fairly extensive goods yard, whereas Wennington had little in the way of goods facilities, concentrating on the passenger traffic associated with a busy junction. Hornby station was closed to passengers and goods on 16th September 1957 and 20th April 1964, respectively. (Robert Humm coll.)

CATON

11. In this undated view, looking west towards Caton, is the former crossing keeper's lodge; the crossing was removed on 5th April 1967. Travel west along the A683 and the building can still be seen on the right when approaching Caton. (CRA)

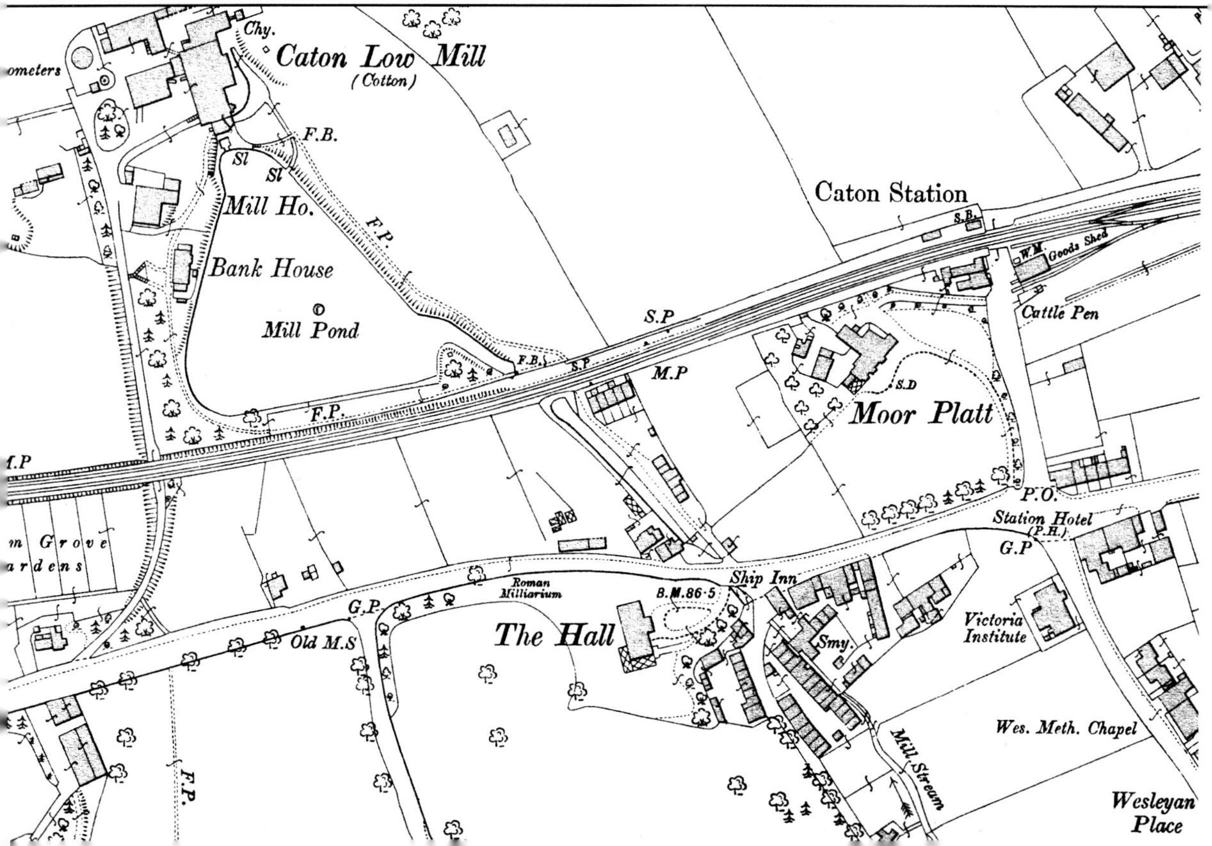

12. After passing the aforementioned sites of the long removed Claughton station and industrial sidings, the next stop on the line is Caton, which opened on 17th November 1849. This westerly view was taken in 1913. (Roy F. Burrows Midland Collection Trust/KRM)

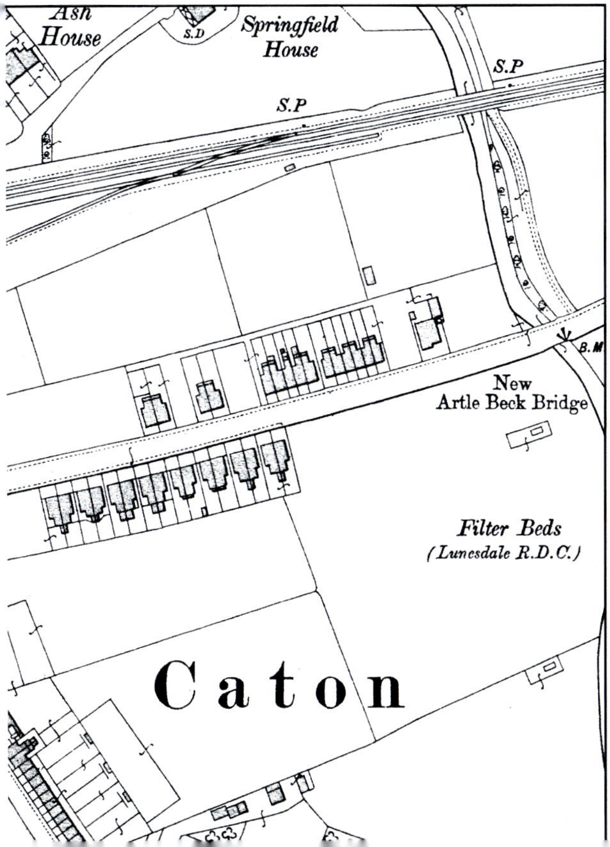

IV. This 1913 map shows the station lying just to the north of the village. To the east of the station, the goods shed sidings and cattle pens can be seen. Further to the east stood Claughton station opened in November 1949; it closed in May 1853. A private siding serving the nearby brickworks was laid soon after the 1923 Grouping.

In the early 1960s a local priest was looking for premises for the growing number of parishioners in Caton. With the help of the then MP, the former goods shed was acquired and converted into a church. In December 1963, Our Lady Immaculate Catholic Church was dedicated.

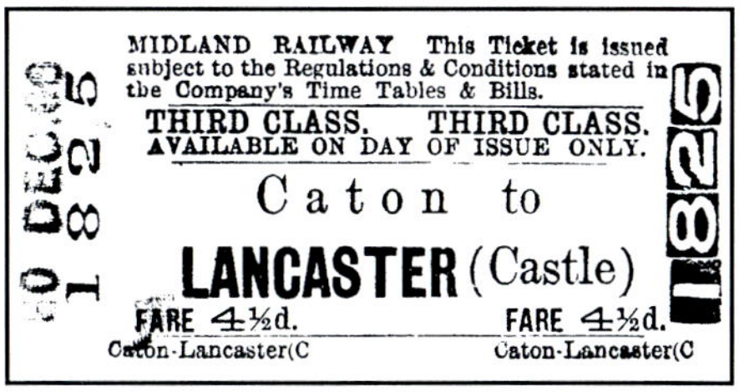

13. In this undated photo, Black 5 no. 44877 is on a down service, passing the signal box and crossing. (CRA)

14. The station was closed to both passengers and goods on 1st May 1961. This view from the forecourt of the station was taken on 3rd January 1966. The former station building had become a private dwelling and remains so to this day. The rendered single-storey frontage of the station house is built in 'Cottage Ornee' style. The section of former line going west is now a popular cycle and pedestrian path into Lancaster and part of the Way of the Roses. (Gordon Biddle/KRM)

WEST OF CATON

Crook O'Lune Viaducts

V. A little to the west of Caton, the line crosses a loop in the river known as the Crook O'Lune. The two viaducts opened on 2nd June 1889, and comprised sandstone piers supporting iron arches - six on the west viaduct and five on the east. Both structures were Grade II listed in November 1983. The 1913 map is scaled at approximately 20ins to 1 mile.

15. On 3rd October 1964, Black 5 no. 45063 hauls the 2.50pm Heysham Harbour to Stourton yard freight across the eastern viaduct, heading towards Caton. The viaducts, that are beautiful examples of Victorian engineering and architecture, remain in place today and carry the aforementioned cycleway and footpath across the Lune. (Noel Machell)

HALTON

16. Royston-based ex-WD/LMS Stanier 8F 2-8-0 no. 48067 heads the 12.40pm empty tank train from Heysham Moss Sidings to Tees Yard through the level crossing to the west side of Halton station on 24th September 1964. To the left of the picture can be seen a noticeboard setting out the toll charges for using the railway-owned bridge (starting with *Cycles 1d*), leading from the station across the River Lune to Halton village. (Noel Machell)

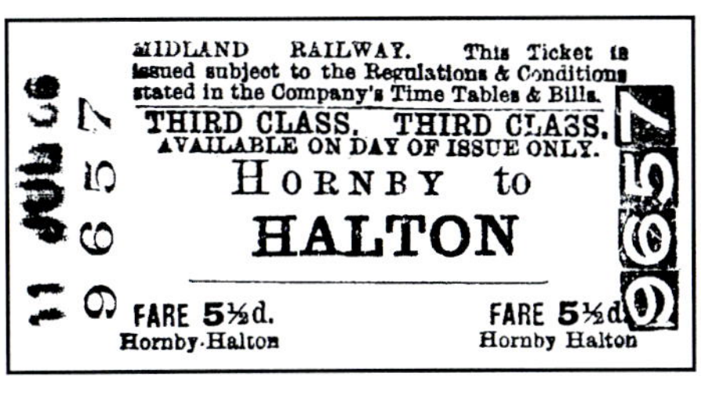

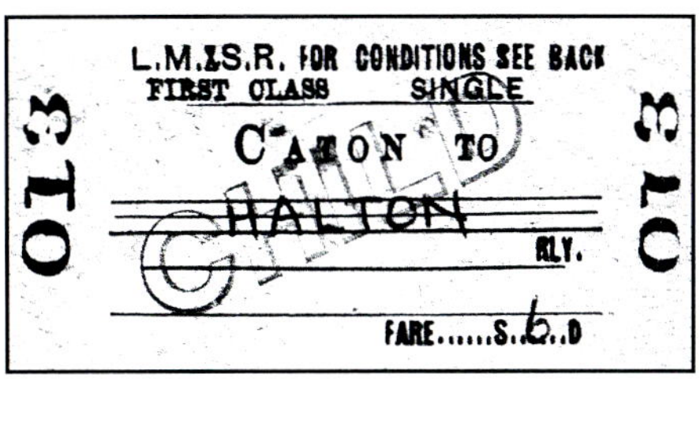

17. Initially, the station was reached by way of a ferry, but severe flooding led to the loss of eight lives. This possibly precipitated the building of the first bridge of timber construction completed in December 1849, soon after the station opened. It was washed away in 1869 and was replaced by a further wooden structure, until eventually being superseded by a more robust bridge made of iron-work from the old Greyhound Bridge in Lancaster. The crossing is known locally as 'Halton Bridge', 'The Iron Bridge', 'Denny Beck Bridge' or 'The Penny Bridge'. Here it is seen on 2nd August 1979.
(John Marshall coll./KRM)

18. Halton station, like others along the route, was opened on 17th November 1849. In this undated photo - possibly early 1920s - a platform level view of the rebuilt station shows three members of staff posing next to the MR running-in board.
(Robert Humm coll.)

VI. This 1913 map clearly shows the River Lune separating the village and station. In April 1907 the original station was destroyed when a spark from the loco of a passing boat train ignited a wagon of oil drums in the yard. The local fire brigade was unable to cross the narrow Penny Bridge and so railway workers were sent from Lancaster to extinguish the fire by passing buckets of water from the river.

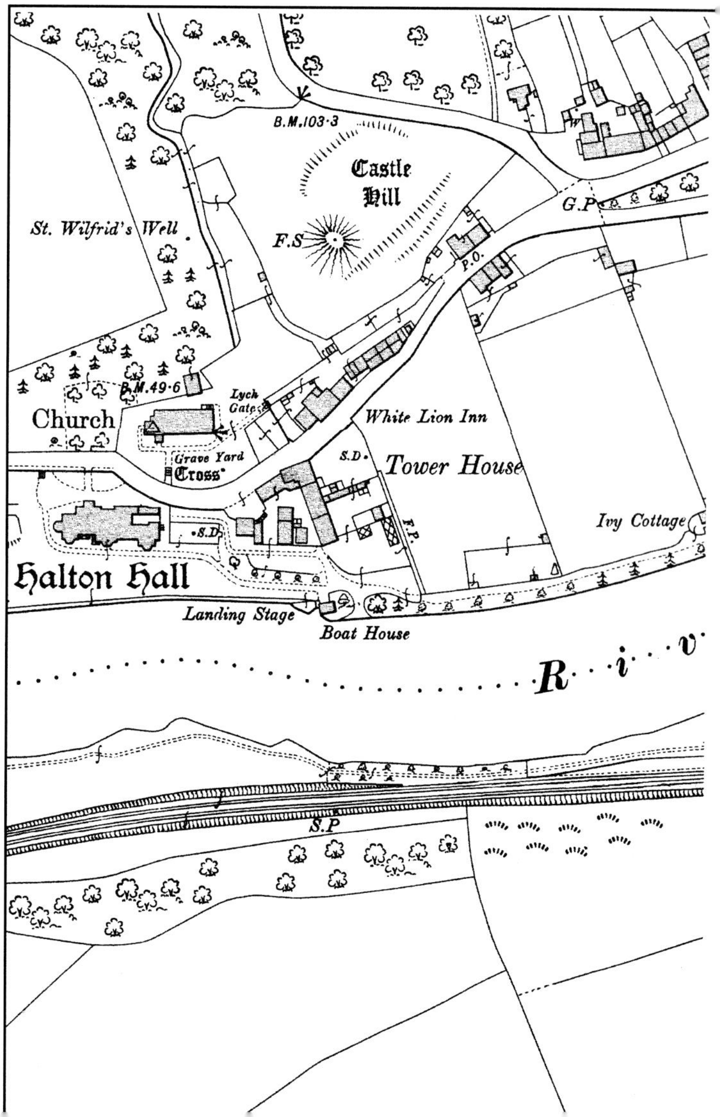

HALTON

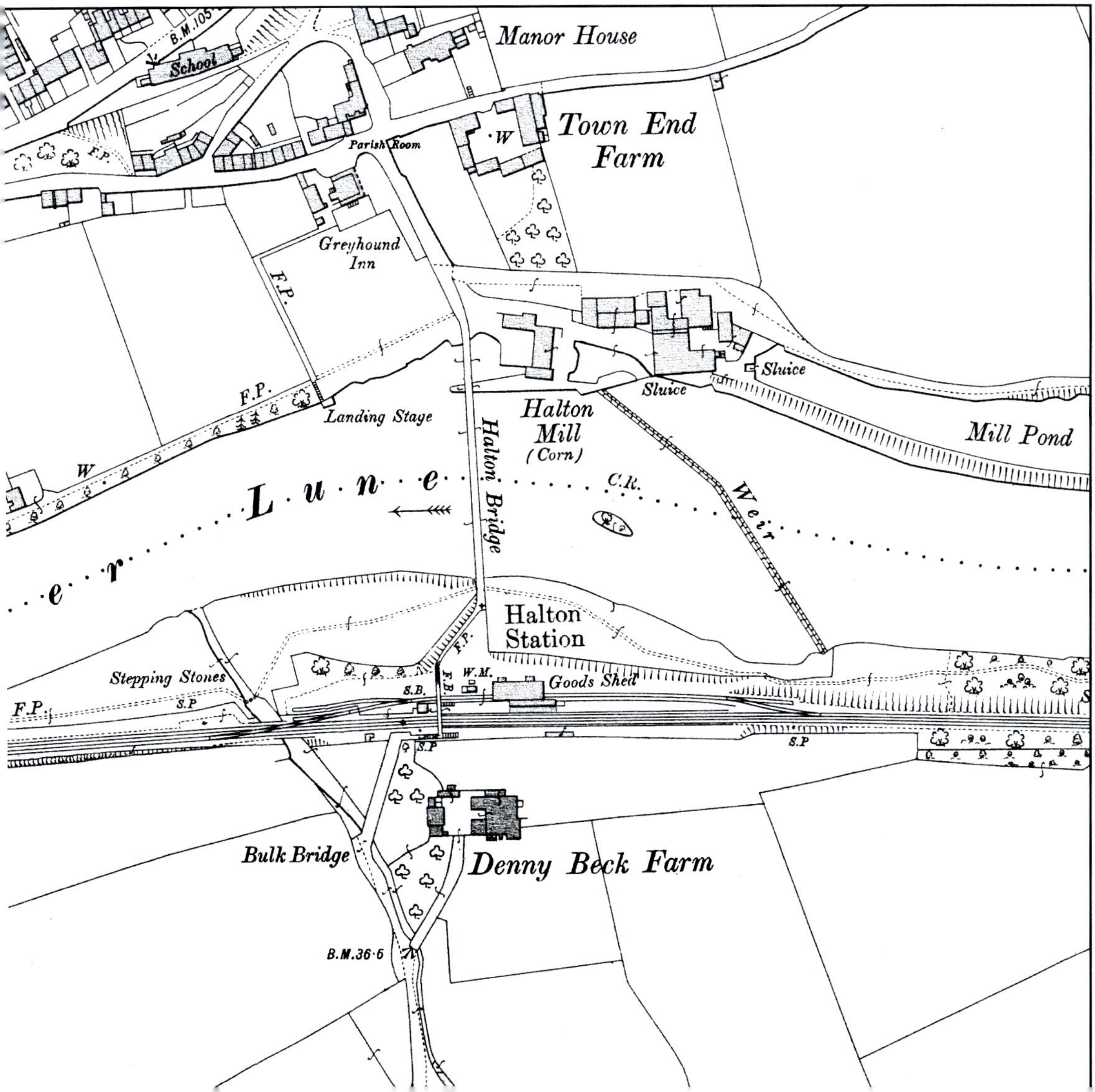
Manor House
B.M.105
School
Town End Farm
W
Parish Room
F.P.
Greyhound Inn
F.P.
Sluice
Sluice
F.P.
Landing Stage
Halton Mill (Corn)
Halton Bridge
Mill Pond
W
L·u·n·e
C.R.
Weir
e·r
Halton Station
Stepping Stones
F.P.
S.B.
W.M.
Goods Shed
F.P.
S.P
F.B.
S.P
S.P
Bulk Bridge
Denny Beck Farm
B.M.36·6

19. A panoramic view of Halton station looking east in 1954. (CRA)

20. A stopping service, hauled by Black 5 no. 44758, draws to a standstill in this undated photo to pick up a small group of waiting passengers. The locomotive, built in 1947, was fitted with Timken roller bearings and was transferred to Lancaster depot in June 1962, where it remained until the shed closed in April 1966. (Noel Machell)

21. A stranger in the camp, in the form of York-allocated ex-LNER (BR 5MT) Thompson B1 4-6-0 no. 61021 *Reitbok*, heads back towards Yorkshire through Halton station. It is hauling the 12.40pm empty tank train from Heysham Moss Sidings to Tees Yard on 25th September 1964. (Noel Machell)

22. The station building is seen on 25th October 1988, long after it was closed to goods in November 1962 and passengers on 3rd January 1966, but the station was not demolished. It is now home to the Lancaster University Boat Club and accommodates the cycleway and footpath; part of the Way of the Roses. (CRA)

APPROACHING LANCASTER

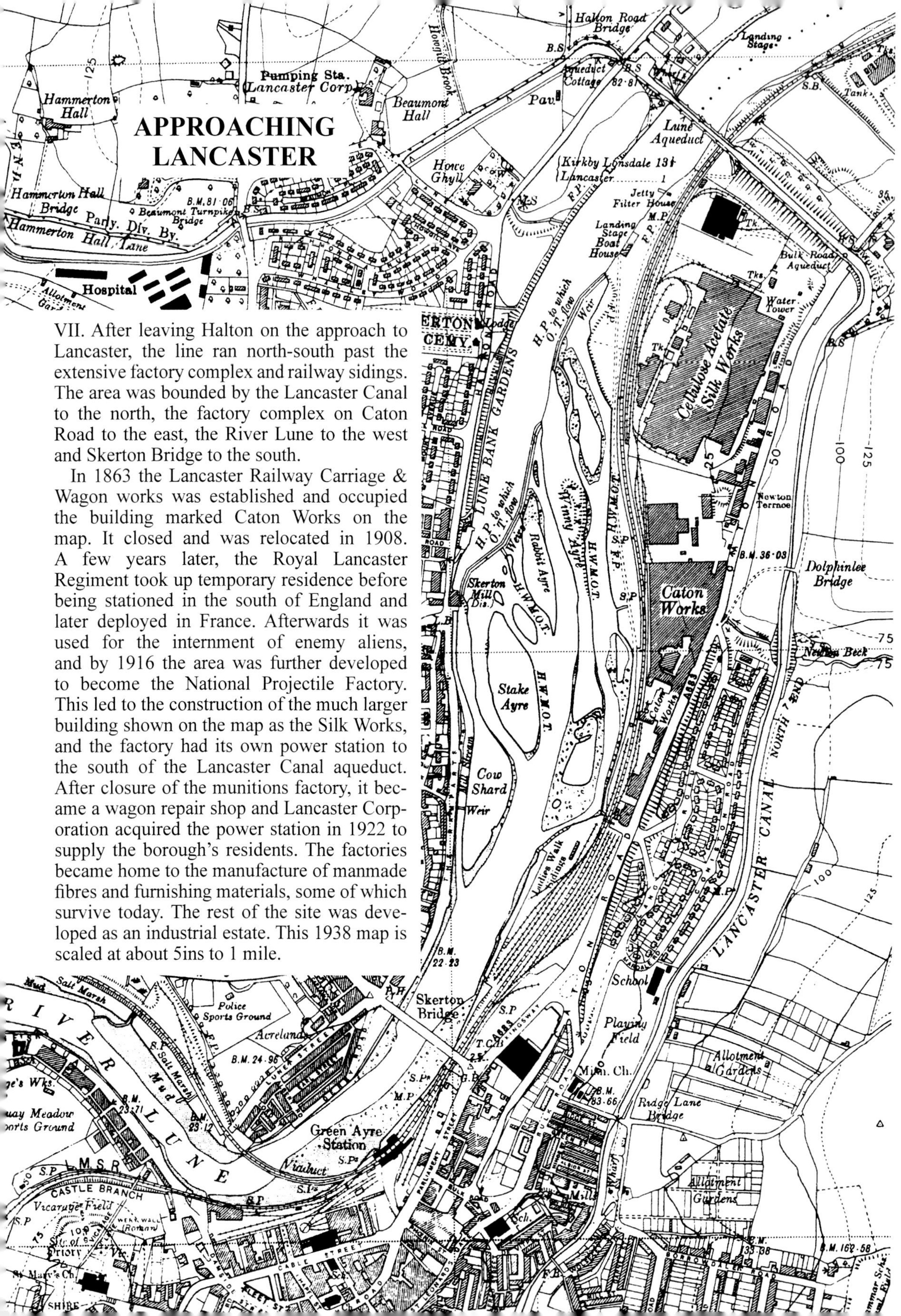

VII. After leaving Halton on the approach to Lancaster, the line ran north-south past the extensive factory complex and railway sidings. The area was bounded by the Lancaster Canal to the north, the factory complex on Caton Road to the east, the River Lune to the west and Skerton Bridge to the south.

In 1863 the Lancaster Railway Carriage & Wagon works was established and occupied the building marked Caton Works on the map. It closed and was relocated in 1908. A few years later, the Royal Lancaster Regiment took up temporary residence before being stationed in the south of England and later deployed in France. Afterwards it was used for the internment of enemy aliens, and by 1916 the area was further developed to become the National Projectile Factory. This led to the construction of the much larger building shown on the map as the Silk Works, and the factory had its own power station to the south of the Lancaster Canal aqueduct. After closure of the munitions factory, it became a wagon repair shop and Lancaster Corporation acquired the power station in 1922 to supply the borough's residents. The factories became home to the manufacture of manmade fibres and furnishing materials, some of which survive today. The rest of the site was developed as an industrial estate. This 1938 map is scaled at about 5ins to 1 mile.

23. In this undated photo, Johnson 1400 class 2-4-0 1409 (later renumbered by the MR and again by the LMS) is seen hauling a newly-built rake of District Railway B stock from the carriage works. These were introduced on to the London Underground network following the use of electric traction on all passenger services, by the end of 1905. Deliveries of stock were made during 1904-05, which indicates an approximate date for the photo. Some of these locomotives remained in service until 1949. (King's Own Royal Regiment Museum, Lancaster)

24. In this photo, taken on 2nd August 1916, the munitions factory complex can be seen in the background; hence the military personnel on the footbridge. The Ladies Walk footbridge, from which other photos in the album were taken, remained in place until the line closed. The signal gantry seen in the distance, to the left of the bridge, controlled entry to the temporary island platform used by workers at the factory - see map VIIIb, on the following page. (CRA)

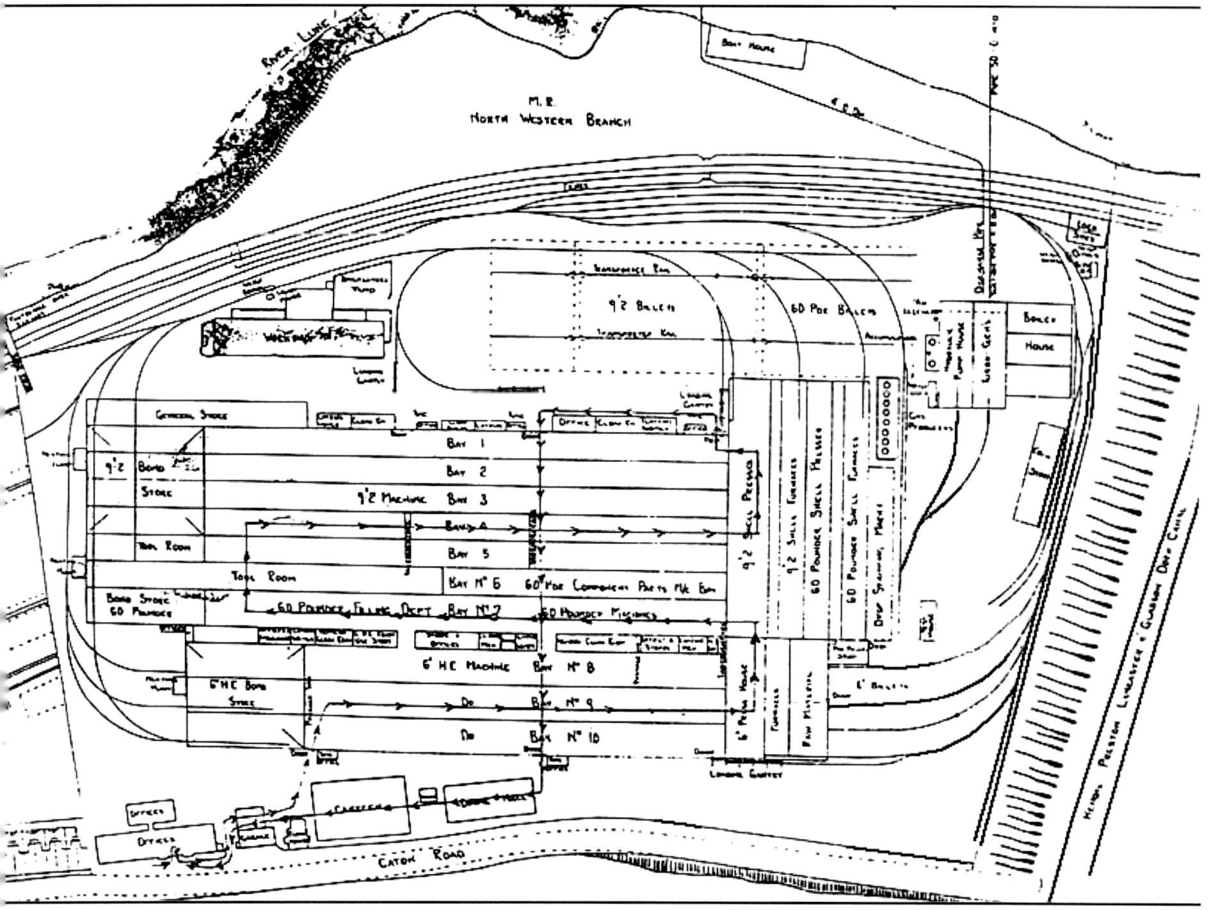

VIIIa. This detailed map shows the standard gauge network within the National Projectile Factory, which was referred to as the Ladies Walk Factory. With no explosives on site, it is unlikely there were any fireless locos at the factory, that is until the two locos were brought in to work at the power station. (King's Own Royal Regiment Museum, Lancaster)

VIIIb. This is a diagram of the layout and associated signalling in connection with the temporary platform, also known as Ladies Walk. It was for workers of the munitions factory, which was on the opposite side of the tracks. Access was via the footbridge. The unshaded bridge to the right of the diagram is that illustrated in picture 24 and the location from where pictures 25, 26 and 27 were taken. (Midland Railway Study Centre, Derby)

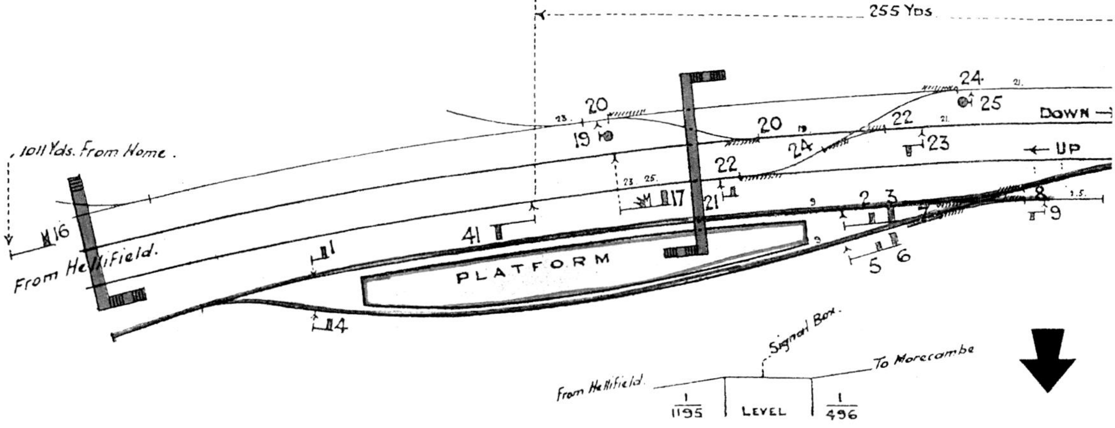

25. Jubilee no. 45564 *New South Wales* passes Ladies Walk Sidings, working 2N71 7.17pm Morecambe Promenade to Leeds City on 30th July 1963. New Zealand sidings can be seen on the left. (Ron Herbert)

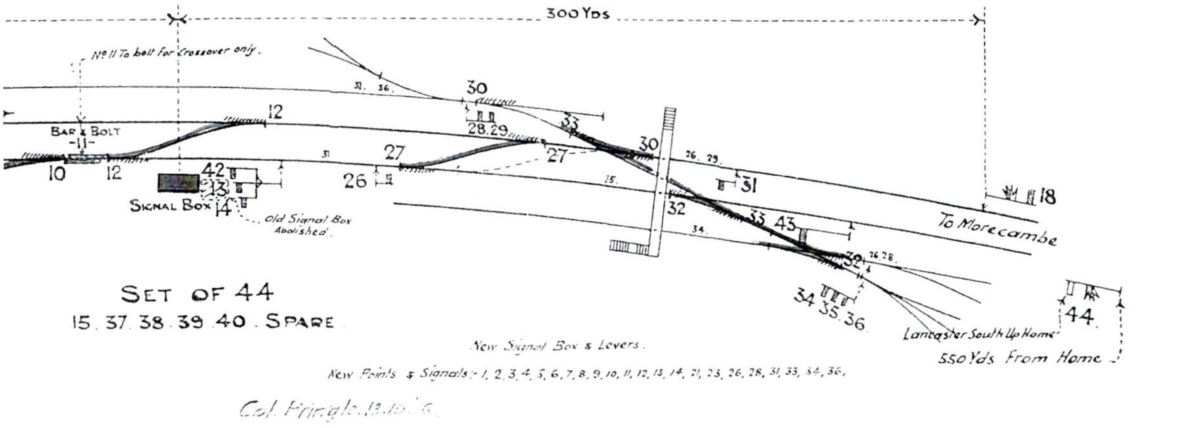

26. An early evening view, on 27th May 1963, from the footbridge at Ladies Walk, shows the rail-served industrial units over on the right. Also on the right, ex-LMS Fowler 3F 0-6-0T no. 47662, also known as a Jinty, heads a trip composed mainly of empty coal wagons from Lancaster CEGB generating station to Lancaster Castle yards. On the left-hand side of the picture, a similar 0-6-0T, no. 47375, stands in the headshunt to Ladies Walk yard with a string of wagons. The signal box was the second replacement, which opened on 25th June 1916 and closed on 4th June 1967. The listed clock tower can be seen between the two chimneys on the right. Note also that any trace of the temporary island platform was long gone by then. (Noel Machell)

➔ 27. Class 25 diesel no. D5206 heads the 9.33am Morecambe-Leeds on 25th September 1964; the freight on the down line is bound for Heysham Harbour. A significant proportion of the traffic in the New Zealand sidings to the left was made up of coal for industrial, commercial, domestic and railway use. Ladies Walk sidings were often used for assembling freight trains bound for Yorkshire. In addition, the Civil Engineers Department occupied some space in this yard in connection with the use of the old dock at Heysham Harbour as its tip, which is now lost under the nuclear power station. (Noel Machell)

28. The two fireless locomotives are on shed at Lancaster generating station. Both were by Andrew Barclay; the leading one is 0-6-0F *Lancaster* AB 1572/1917, and the other 0-4-0F AB 1950/1928. Following closure of the facility in August 1976 both locos were transferred to Heysham Nuclear Power Station in October 1977. The edifice visible in the background is the famous listed stone-built aqueduct for the Lancaster Canal crossing over the River Lune and its adjoining flood plains. The architect was John Rennie, famous for many works, including London's Waterloo Bridge inspired by his design of Skerton Bridge in Lancaster. (Fred Butler/KRM)

29. *Lancaster* hauls wagons through the power station on Caton Road in the late 1960s. Coal trains were usually brought in by a BR shunter through a gate near the Lansil factory and stockpiled in sidings on the other side of the canal. Coal wagons were then taken into the power station by the two fireless locos as needed. Just visible in the distance is the line from Wennington to Lancaster. (Keith Wilkinson)

LANCASTER GREEN AYRE

30. This exterior shot of Green Ayre station was taken on 6th April 1966, shortly after the line closed to passenger traffic, although freight traffic through the station continued until 1967. The station was rebuilt in 1873 not long after acquisition by the MR to a design by Edmund Sharpe, sometime partner of E.G.Paley. Until 1st November 1870, timetables incorrectly listed the station as 'Lancaster Green Area'. Visitors today will understand the irony of that error; all that remains is a green area between the two road bridges on which stands a crane from the nearby former Hornby goods yard and commemorative stone to mark the spot. (J Tolson/*Colour-Rail.com*)

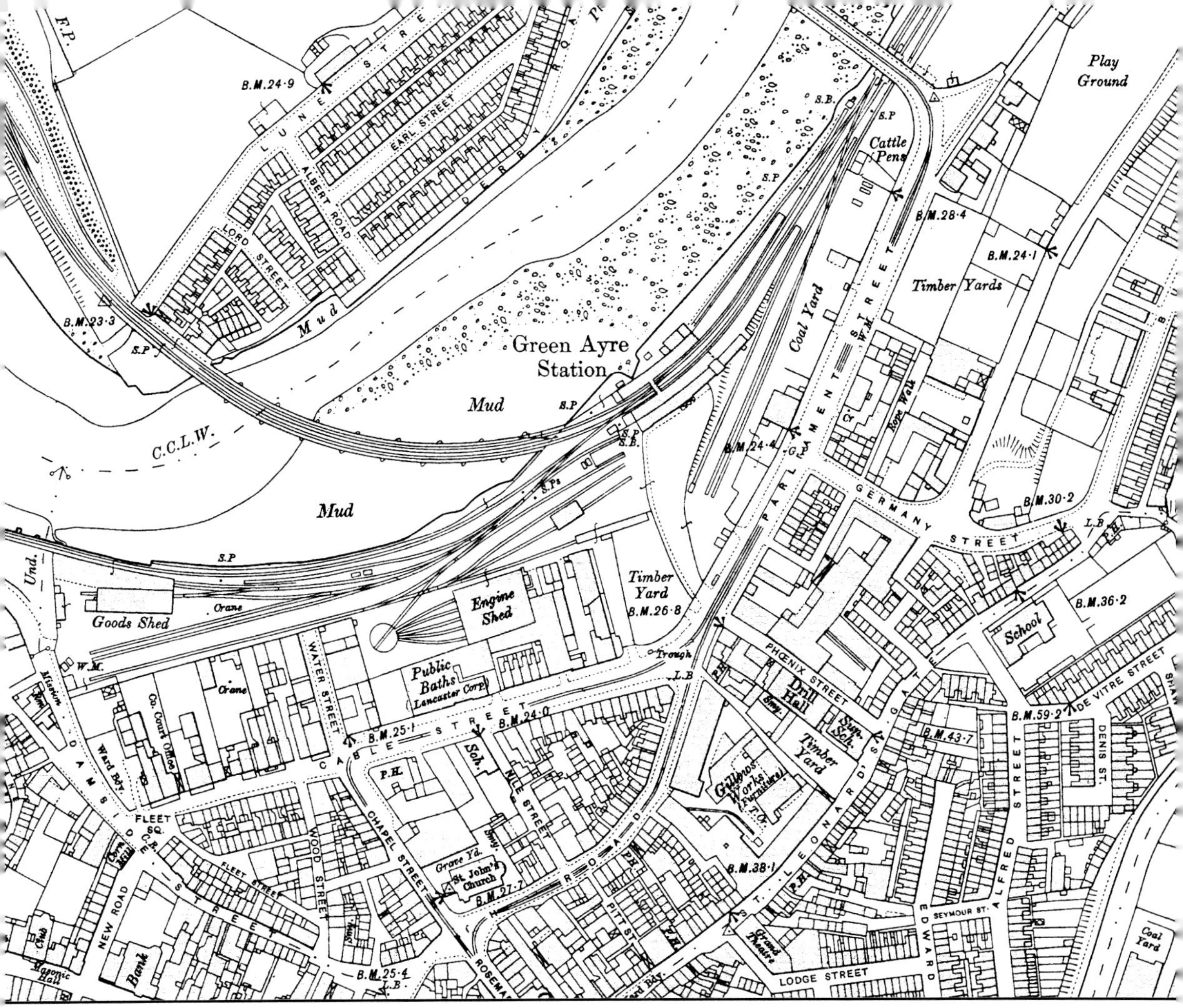

IX. This 20ins to 1 mile map of the rebuilt Green Ayre station is dated 1913. The coal yard, to the front on Parliament Street, would have extended up to the fence, near where the Ford Anglia is parked in picture no.30. The bay platform is on the north side of the station; it was used for stopping services to Skipton and Leeds. At the south end of the station, three lines emerge: veering off to the right is the mainline to Morecambe/Heysham via the Greyhound Bridge; the line in the middle of the three is the spur to Lancaster Castle station and, straight ahead is the line to the motive power depot and goods shed. Note that entry to the engine shed was via the turntable only.

The word 'ayre' is derived from the Old Norse 'eyrr', meaning a shingle beach or gravelly place; as in the names of several shingle banks, namely: Salt Ayre; Whinny Ayre; Stake Ayre; Rabbit Ayre and Green Ayre, in the tidal reach of the River Lune at Lancaster.
(Rev. R. Farnworth Railways Blog)

July 1903

LANCASTER and MORECAMBE.—Midland.

Miles	Down. Green Ayre,	Week Days.																															
		mrn	mrn	mrn	mrn	mrn	mrn	mrn	mrn	aft	aft	aft	aft	a	a	c	aft	a	b	aft	aft	a	aft	aft	aft	aft	aft	aft	aft	aft			
—	Lancaster ....dep.	6 0	6 30	7 5	8 15	8 53	9 34	11 9	1119	12 5	1234	1259	1 19	1 39	2 14	2 18	2 44	3 4	3 20	3 59	4 24	4 34	5 45	5 59	6 44	7 34	7 58	9 9	1015	1045	....	....	....
3¼	Morecambe ......arr.	6 6	6 36	7 12	8 21	9 0	9 40	1115	1125	1211	1240	1 5	1 25	1 45	2 20	2 25	2 50	3 10	3 26	4 5	4 30	4 40	5 51	6 5	6 50	7 40	8 5	9 15	1022	1052	....	....	....
Mls	Up.	mrn	mrn	mrn	mrn	mrn	mrn	mrn	mrn	mrn	aft	aft	aft	aft	a	aft	aft	aft	aft	aft	aft	aft	aft	aft	aft	aft	aft	a	aft				
—	Morecambe ......dep.	6 15	6 45	7 5	7 58	8 15	8 30	9 50	11 5	1140	1215	1 15	2 30	3 5	3 50	4 0	4 30	5 15	5 40	6 10	6 35	6 50	7 30	8 5	9 10	9 55	1030	1040	11 0	....	....	....	....
3¼	Lancaster 539 ..arr.	6 21	6 51	7 11	8 4	8 22	8 36	9 56	1111	1146	1221	1 21	2 36	3 12	3 56	4 6	4 36	5 21	5 46	6 16	6 41	6 56	7 36	8 12	9 16	10 2	1036	1046	11 6	....	....	....	....

Down. Green Ayre,	Sundays.											
	mrn	mrn	mrn	mrn	mrn	aft	aft	aft	aft	aft	aft	
Lancaster ....dep.	8 0	9 14	9 34	9 44	9 59	2 45	5 30	6 30	7 40	8 50	9 50	....
Morecambe *(side)* ....arr.	8 6	9 20	9 40	9 50	10 5	2 52	5 36	6 36	7 46	8 56	9 56	....

Up.	Sundays.													
	mrn	mrn	mrn	aft	aft	aft	aft	aft	aft	aft	aft			
Morecambe ....dep.	8 25	9 50	1030	5 0	6 0	6 40	6 55	7 5	8 25	9 30	1010	....	....	....
Lancaster *(side)* ....arr	8 32	9 56	1036	5 6	6 6	6 46	7 2	7 11	8 32	9 36	1016	....	....	....

a Saturdays only. **b** Except Saturdays. **c** Wednesdays only.

31. Electrification work is in progress at Green Ayre in 1908. The two lines to the left lead towards the Greyhound Bridge and on to Morecambe and Heysham. To the right, the line leads to the motive power depot, goods shed and the spur to Lancaster Castle. The signal box was known as the North box, even though it was geographically south of the South box at the far end of the platform. (J. Alsop coll.)

32. In this 1925 photo of Green Ayre and its North signal box is 1400 class 2-4-0 no. 211, a Johnson design, which entered traffic as no.1404 in 1879, with 211 being its 1907 number. It was withdrawn in October 1934. It was a Carnforth engine in 1920 and the Midland shed at Carnforth closed in 1934; so, its withdrawal date may not be coincidental. (J. Alsop coll.)

33. An early undated shot shows a two-car EMU departing from Green Ayre. These units were referred to as 'Leccies' by local passengers. The North signal box, situated behind the front of the train, was closed on 13th March 1932 and later demolished. (Robert Humm coll.)

34. Ex-LNER B1 no. 61020 *Gemsbok* hauls a Leeds-Morecambe excursion on 18th April 1960. The train is seen passing the South box referred to earlier. The coaches for a local train to Skipton and Leeds can be seen in the bay platform. (CRA Pearsall coll.)

2N 71

45643

← 35. Hauling a short train of four coaches, BR Sulzer 'Peak' 1Co-Co1 no. D25 pulls away from Lancaster Green Ayre station with the 7.17pm Morecambe–Leeds train on 27th May 1963. The two coaches stabled in the bay will form the following morning's 8.05am Lancaster-Leeds stopping train. The Parliament Street coal/goods yard is visible behind the first and second coach; it was taken out of use on 7th October 1968. (Noel Machell)

↙ 36. Jubilee 4-6-0 no. 45643 *Rodney* steams through Green Ayre with the 14.50 Heysham-Stourton Goods on Christmas Eve 1965. (CRA Pearsall coll.)

↓ 37. A forlorn-looking Green Ayre station is pictured on 24th February 1975. The single line passing through it is the remains of the spur from Lancaster Castle station leading to the power station. It was taken out of use on 17th March 1976 and the station was demolished later that year. (Michael Ellis)

Lancaster Motive Power Depot

38. Lancaster MPD running shed is seen on 5th July 1947. The shed code changed over the years during MR, LMS and, later, BR control. (Robert Humm coll.)

➔ 39. Black 5 no. 44889 was seen at Green Ayre depot on 21st September 1965. It is being coaled with the fireman stood on the tender manhandling a coaling tub. These were loaded from the wagons to the right-hand side of the building and then elevated to the locomotive via an inclined arm; the whole process was heavily dependent on a great deal of elbow grease. (Noel Machell)

➔ 40. The same locomotive runs on to the depot turntable for turning after being coaled. The radiating road on the extreme left gave access to a short line latterly used to store locomotives awaiting disposal, and the next four roads led into the depot, The shed closed on 18th April 1966 and the site of the former MPD is now occupied by a large retail superstore. (Noel Machell)

44889

Lancaster Castle Spur

41. This September 1964 photo shows EMU M29023M having descended from Lancaster Castle into Green Ayre, where it would have reversed and continued on to Morecambe. Apart from the Castle and Priory and surroundings in the background, almost everything else in this picture was associated with the railway and has long gone save for the Greyhound Bridge to the right, which carries northbound A6 and local traffic over the River Lune. (Ron Herbert)

42. Another September 1964 shot this time sees EMU M28220M climbing the spur to Lancaster Castle. In the background is the Greyhound Bridge and, beyond that, Lancaster Green Ayre station can be seen. The River Lune flows in front of the houses on St George's Quay, behind the train. (Ron Herbert)

43. From almost the exact same spot on 25th September 1964, Jinty no. 47531 coasts down the spur to Green Ayre station with a trip train bound for Ladies Walk yard; the contents of the second and third wagons looking very much like spoil bound for the civil engineers' tip at Heysham Harbour. The gradient on the spur is reported variously as 1 in 70 and 1 in 89; official records show it as 1 in 78, which is probably the average incline over the line. (Noel Machell)

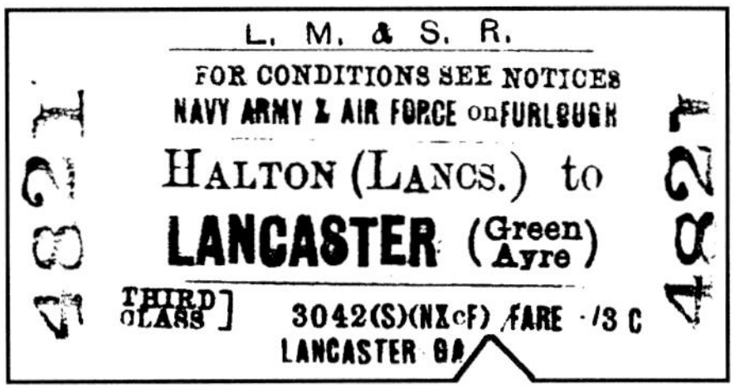

LANCASTER CASTLE

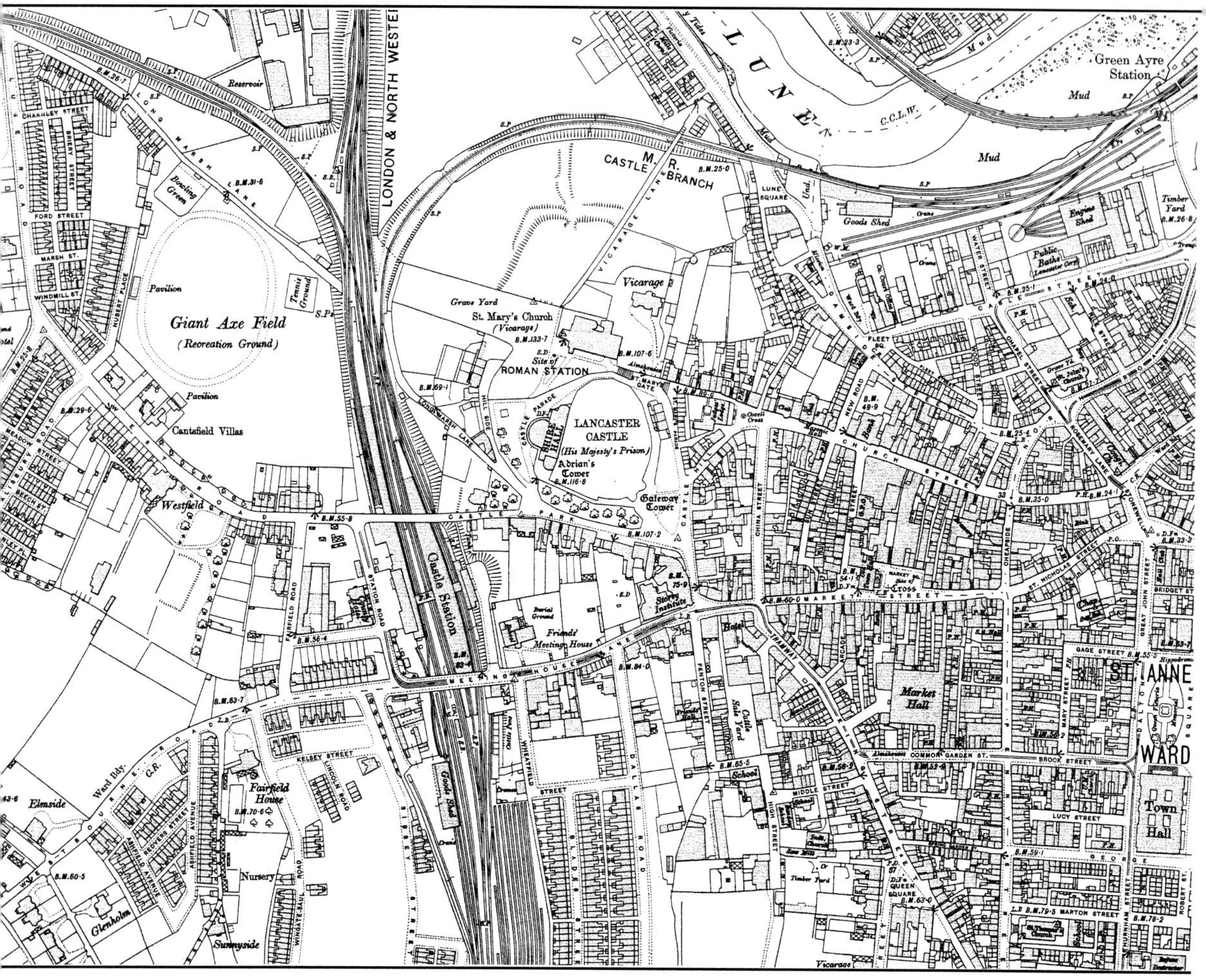

X. This 1913 map, at about 15ins to 1 mile, shows the north end of Lancaster Castle station and the spur to Green Ayre diverging to the right. Ahead is the main line to Carlisle and Glasgow and, to the left, is the former Glasson Dock branch. In two dimensions, the map does not indicate the gradient on the Lancaster Castle spur, whereas it is very apparent in the photographs.

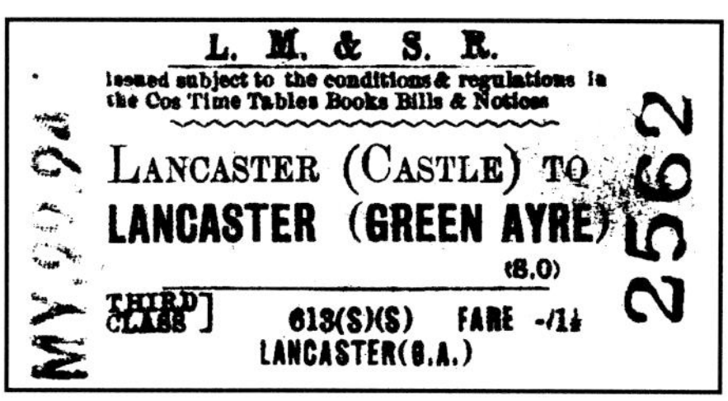

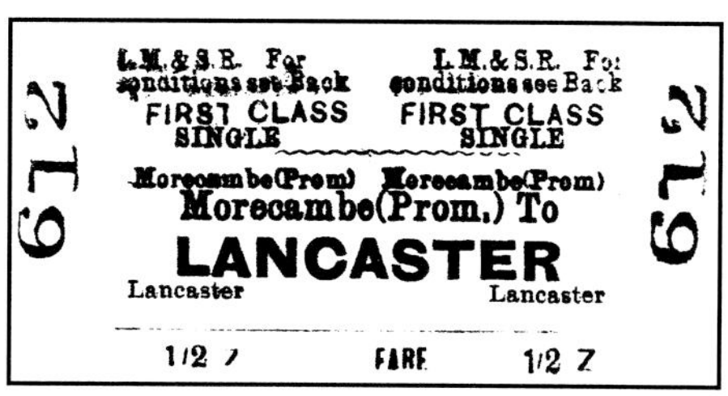

44. EMU M28220M is at the top of the spur in May 1963; the destination is shown as Heysham, so it could well be heading back down the branch to reverse at Green Ayre. In the foreground are the tracks of the WCML. Note the elegant gantries that LNWR insisted on at this point; the company also had custody of a key that would enable it to switch off power to the branch, if required. The key was held at Lancaster No. 4 signal box situated north of Castle station. (*Colour-Rail.com*)

45. A first generation EMU is pictured waiting at platform 6. Constructed by William Tite, the L&CR opened Lancaster Castle station on 22nd September 1846; it was later extended and, in 1900, buildings were constructed on the eastern side, as seen in this picture. Both buildings are Grade II listed. Platform 6 was used by MR electrics from the outset of operations and platform 5, from where this photo was taken, in the 1950s when it was electrified. (J. Alsop coll.)

46. EMU M28221M stands at the now disused platform 6 at Lancaster Castle on 17th June 1956. The track layout in the station area was rationalised in 1973 and this included the removal of the track alongside platform 6, although it had seen no regular use for some time prior to that work being carried out. Driving motor coach 28221 was fitted with a germanium rectifier and displayed at the International Railway Congress, Willesden, London, between 26th and 29th May 1954. (J. Tolson/*Colour-Rail.com*)

47. Services to Morecambe and Heysham via Green Ayre also used platform 5, where Set 20 is standing on 24th December 1965, just days before the end of passenger services over the former MR line. Units were not allocated running numbers, but were identified for drivers' rosters by the last two digits of the driving motor coach - see table opposite. (*Colour-Rail.com*)

48. This was the end as far as electric traction was concerned on the spur and on the former Midland route between Lancaster, Morecambe and Heysham. Here, a wiring train near Lancaster Castle station is removing catenary equipment on 28th June 1966. At this time, the WCML was only electrified as far as Preston. The spur remained open to allow coal to be delivered to Lancaster power station until taken out of use on 17th March 1976. It closed on 1st October the same year. The suffix of 'Castle' had been dropped as from 5th June 1969. (CRA Pearsall coll.)

The AM1s did not have unit numbers but were identified, for driver rosters etc, by the last two numbers of the driving motor coach as can be seen in the table below:

SET	DMBSO	TSO	DTSO
19	M28219M	M29721M	M29021M
20	M28220M	M29722M	M29022M
21	M28221M	M29723M	M29023M
22	M28222M	M29724M	M29024M

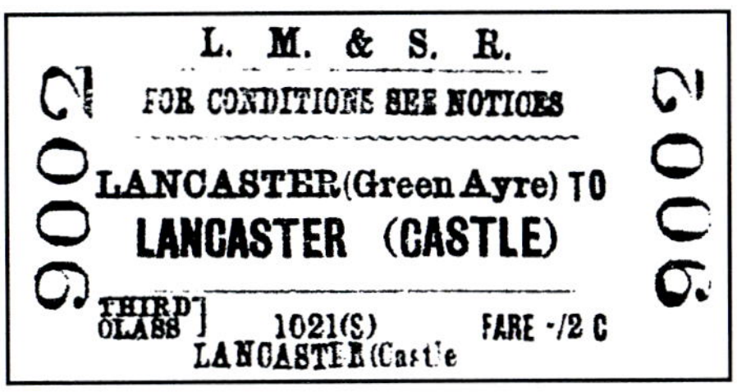

2. Lancaster to Morecambe

Greyhound Bridge to Scale Hall

49. This 1933 photograph shows clearly the rail network in Lancaster. Lower right is Green Ayre station with the line sweeping across the Lune via the iconic Greyhound Bridge towards Morecambe and Heysham. Centre left is Lancaster MPD and goods shed, and, snaking up towards the gasometer, is the spur to Lancaster Castle station that is located behind the castle and priory, top left. The WCML follows the line of trees in front of the gasometer towards Carlisle Bridge, where it crosses the River Lune. The 'first' Greyhound Bridge, mainly built of timber, was completed in 1848. That was then replaced by a wrought iron structure completed in 1864, and again redeveloped in 1911, when the current bridge was constructed. After closure of the line to Morecambe in 1966, the bridge was converted for road traffic and carries the northbound A6 and A589 over the River Lune. After the second rebuild, some of the metalwork was used to construct the Denny Beck bridge at Halton - see picture 17. (Historic England)

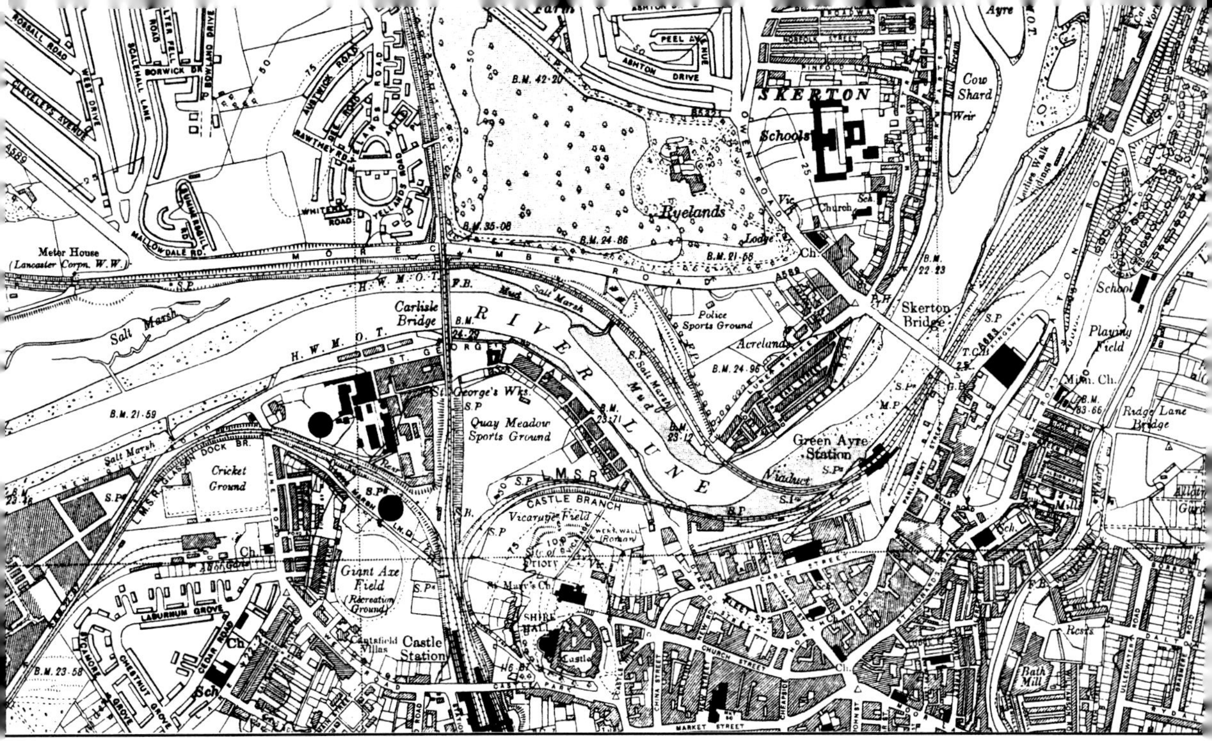

XI. Were it to be turned 90° this 1939 map, at about 4ins to 1 mile, would match the features in the previous photograph. It shows the route to Morecambe having crossed the Lune via the Greyhound Bridge, then passing under the Carlisle Bridge that carries the WCML.

50. The journey proper to the coast starts here. This is an undated photo of an EMU on the Greyhound Bridge. It has just departed Green Ayre station setting off for Morecambe on a frosty day. (Paul Claxton coll.)

51. Ex-LMS Fairburn 4P 2-6-4T no. 42154 of Carnforth depot runs bunker first over Greyhound Bridge with the through coaches for Morecambe, which had been detached earlier at Wennington off the 1.53pm Leeds-Carnforth train on 12th June 1965. (Noel Machell)

52. Here we see single line working introduced in 1908 to allow services to continue while the MR line was being electrified. Unlike the signals, the 'Lune' box was a temporary affair and was removed after completion of the electrification programme on 15th March 1908, some six weeks after being erected. According to the *Midland Railway Journal* no. 39, the train appears to be headed by a Johnson 2-4-0 locomotive travelling westward and about to collect the token for its onward journey. (J. Alsop coll.)

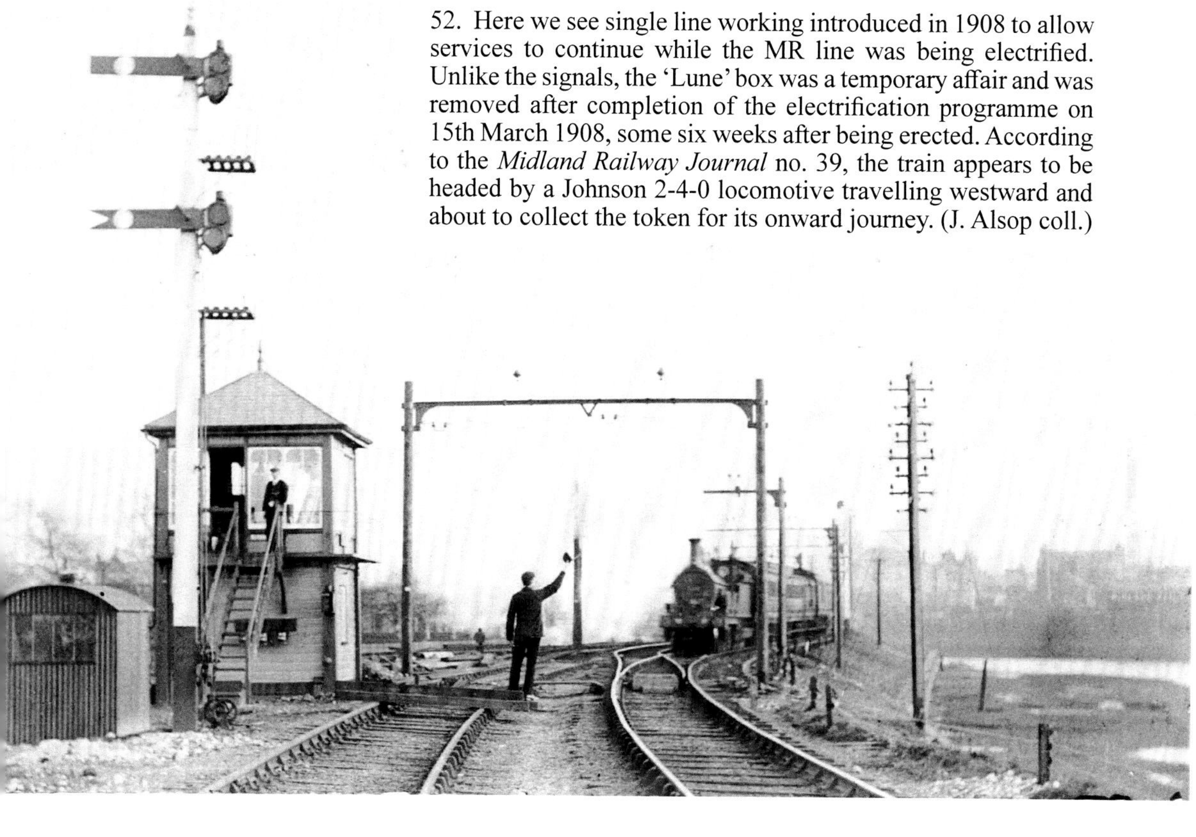

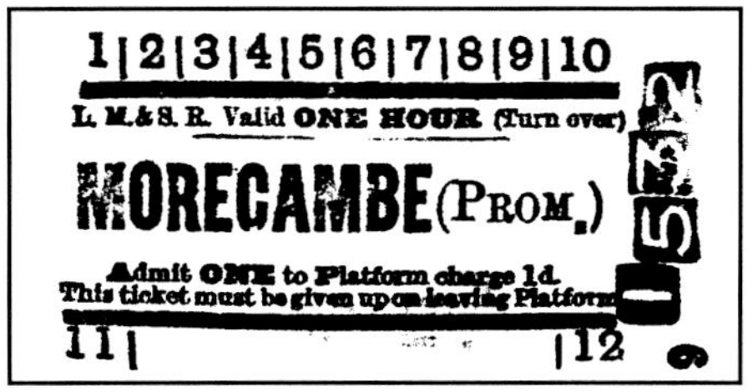

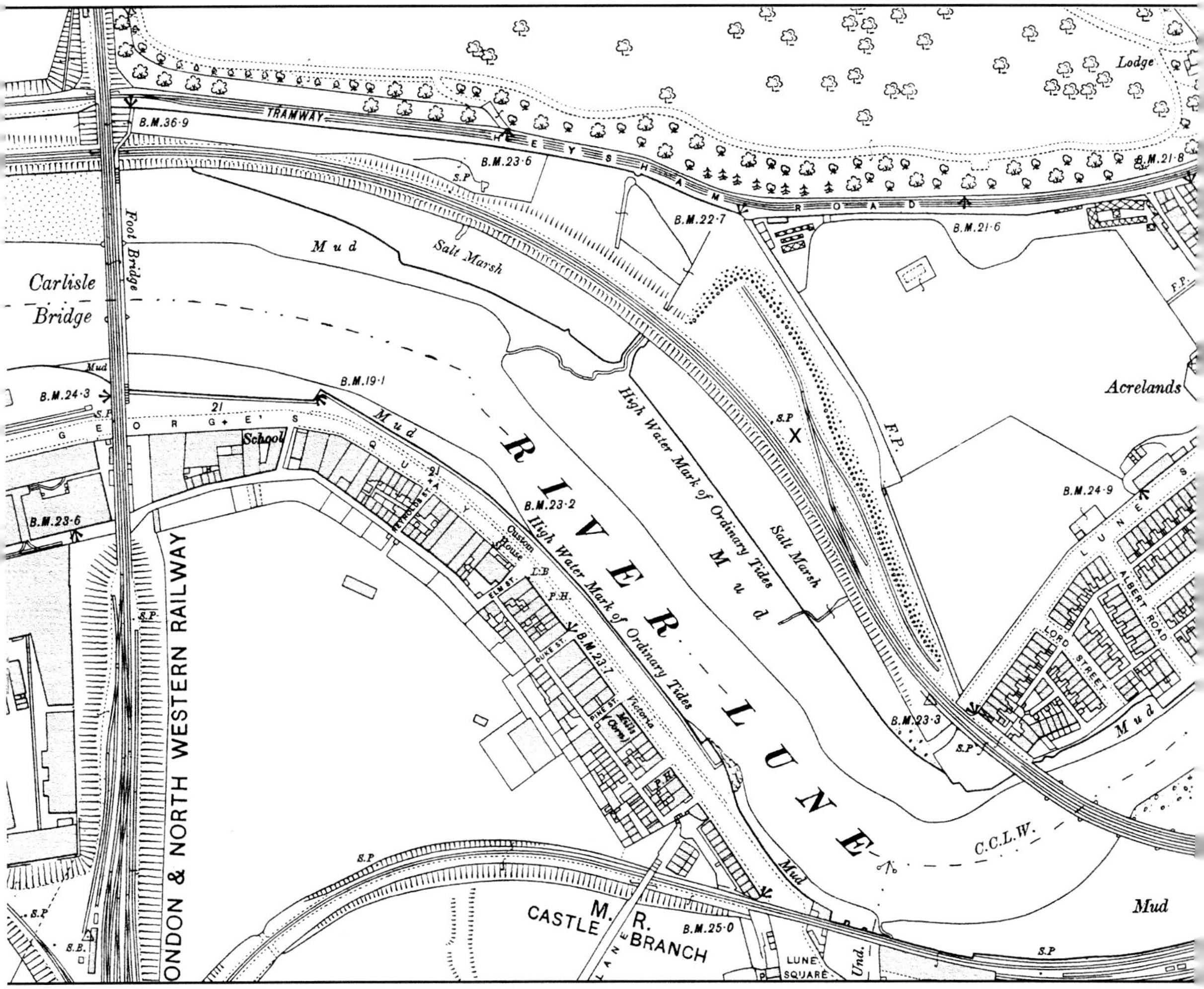

XII. This 1913 map shows the location of the temporary signal box (marked with an 'X') that would have been adjacent to the signal post between the main line and the sidings. They were referred to as the earth sidings and most likely used for civil engineers trains during the electrification of the line. According to OS maps of the time, the sidings appear to have been removed between the 1936 and 1939 editions.

53. EMU Sets 21 (M28221M) and 19 (M28219) work in tandem on the 5.55pm Lancaster-Morecambe service on 1st April 1956. The train has just passed under the Carlisle Bridge. The units were serviced annually at Meols Cop near Southport; they were towed to avoid interference with colour light signalling along with out-of-gauge wing mirrors and running boards being removed for the journey. (CRA Pearsall coll.)

SCALE HALL

54. A shot of the station ticket office was taken on 2nd October 1965. While closure of the line was some way off, when it did come to an end the building was demolished and much of it moved to Morecambe Cricket Club. The old wooden pavilion was replaced by a smart brick-built affair that, externally, as visitors and players will know, bears no resemblance to the station. (J. Tolson/*Colour-Rail.com*)

55. The station opened on 8th June 1957 and closed on 3rd January 1966, when passenger services on the former MR ceased; could this be the shortest lived permanent station on the national network? A former local resident remembers his wife taking advantage of a special 4d 'pram' ticket to Lancaster for mothers with children. It is assumed that mothers returning from Lancaster with prams, toddlers and shopping would have been allowed to use the crossing rather than negotiate the footbridge. This shot was taken on 2nd October 1965, looking back towards Skerton. (J. Tolson/*Colour-Rail.com*)

↑ 56. Scale Hall station is pictured on 23rd September 1964 with driver trailer open second M29023M leading and working 2P96 12.40pm Morecambe Promenade to Lancaster Castle. The station was adjacent to the former Royal Flying Corps airfield. (Ron Herbert)

→ 57. On Saturday 28th October 1961, the return working of the 'Residential Express' left Bradford Forster Square for Morecambe at 12.46pm and was a short train due to the absence of a Leeds portion. In this shot, Jubilee no. 45565 *Victoria*, a long-term resident of Leeds Holbeck depot, heads a four-coach train past Scale Hall. (Noel Machell)

↗ 58. Fowler 4F no. 44570 approaches Scale Hall station working 7N54 12.40pm Heysham Moss to Tees Yard on 24th January 1964. Note the variety of OLE that was being tested along the Golden Mile after the line was re-energised in 1953. (Ron Herbert)

44570

EAST OF MORECAMBE

White Lund Munitions Factory and Gas Works

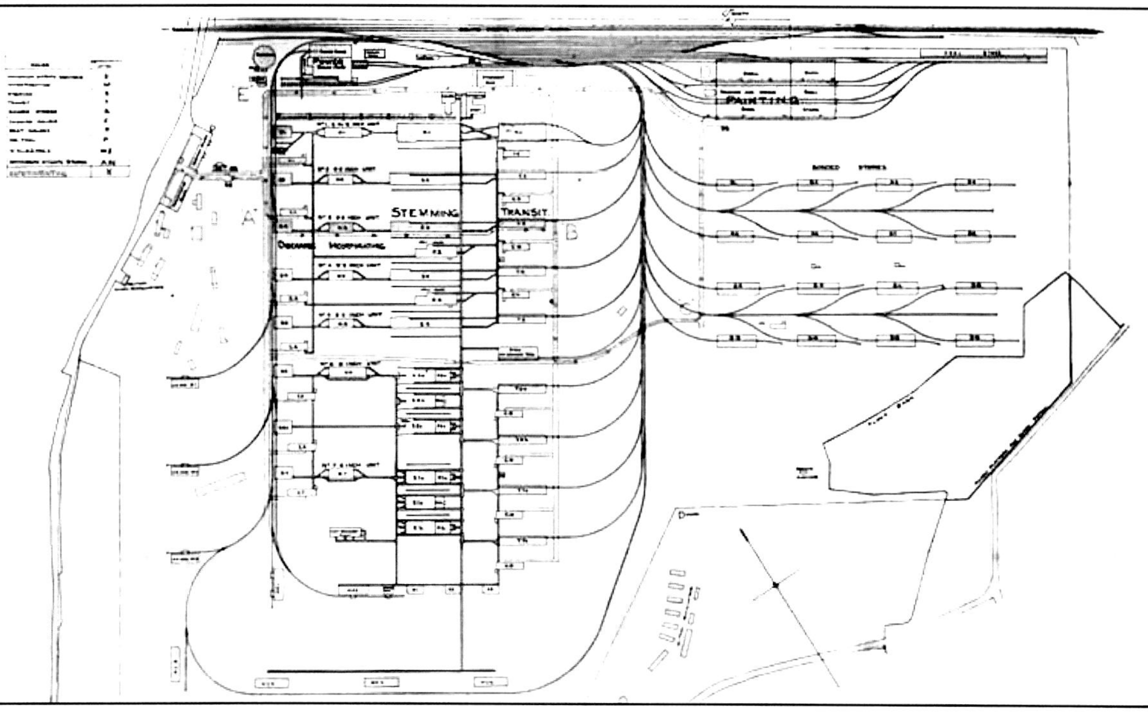

XIIIa. This is a diagram of the standard gauge internal layout at the National Filling Factory No. 13 at White Lund, Morecambe, sometimes referred to as the Torrisholme factory.

In October 1917, following a fire and a number of explosions at the factory, at least four people were killed. By 1919 the remaining buildings were being used to dismantle shells to render them safe, but in January 1920 there was a further explosion, leading to the unfortunate deaths of nine workers. After that, the factory was wound down and later saw the new Morecambe gasworks erected on the site. Since closure of the gasworks, the site has become part of the White Lund trading estate.

Three Andrew Barclay fireless locomotives (works nos. 1471-3) were delivered to the factory in 1916. Two of the locomotives have been preserved: 1472 at Bressingham, awaiting its fate, and 1473, later named *Sir Charles*, is in storage at the Swansea Museum Collection Centre. (King's Own Royal Regiment Museum, Lancaster)

← To the left is an old Morecambe postcard. (Bob Teevan)

XIIIb. This diagram is from the handwritten/drawn MR Signal Alteration Book of 1916. It illustrates the connection to the factory towards Torrisholme junction, sidings adjacent to the main line and the temporary wooden platforms for use by factory workers. (Midland Railway Study Centre, Derby)

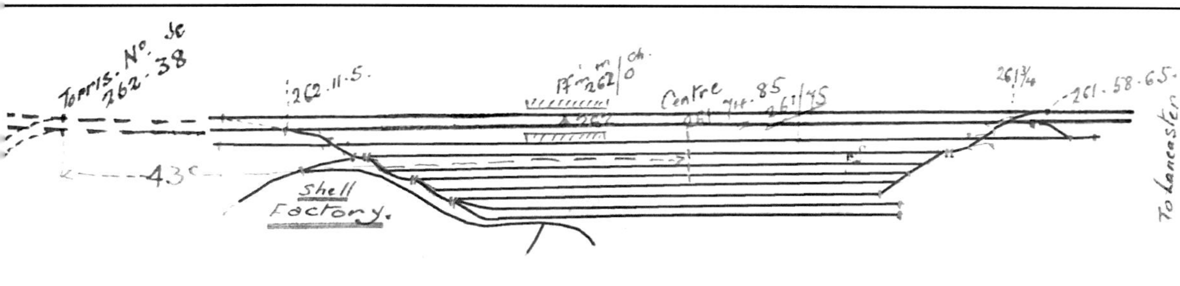

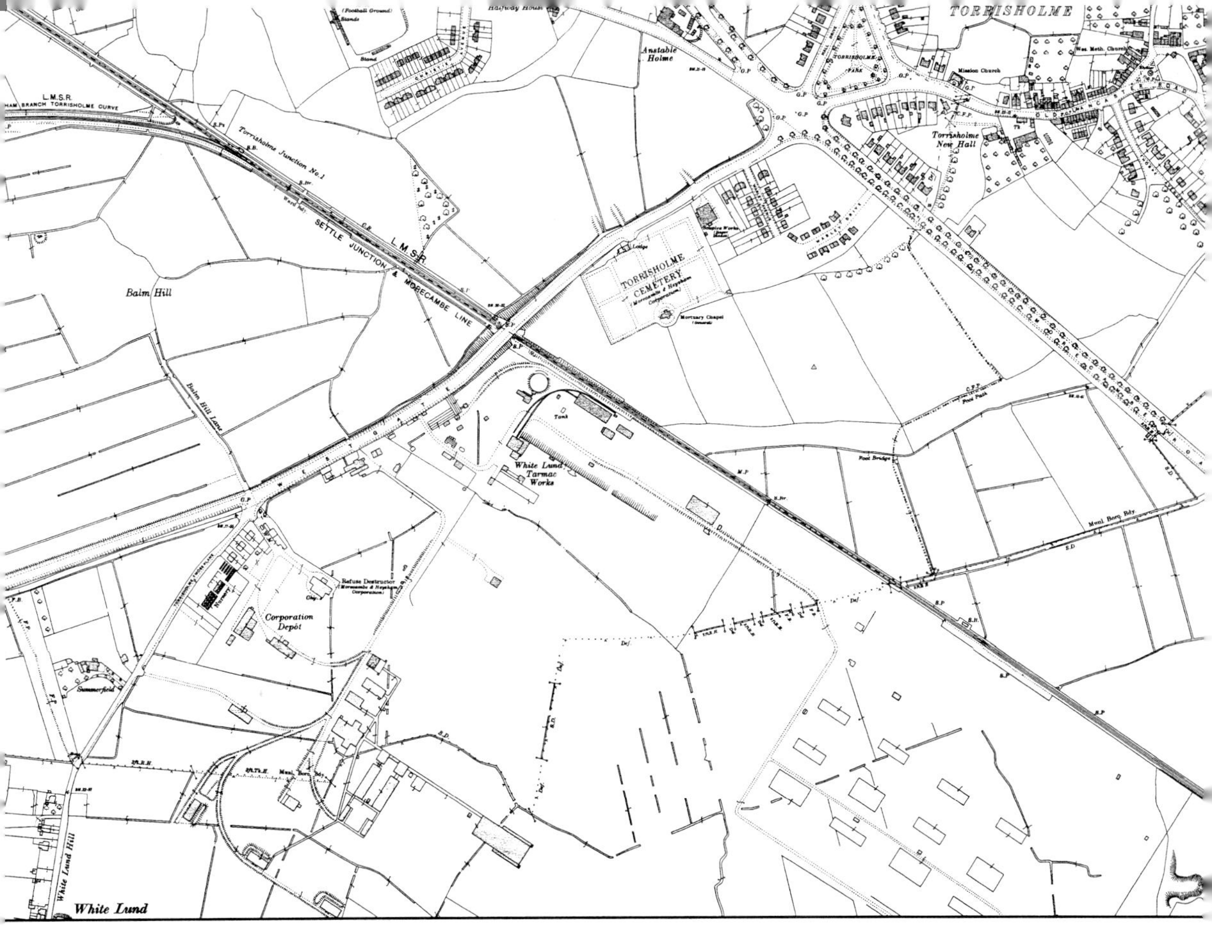

XIIIc. In this 1933 map (scaled at approximately 15ins to 1 mile), the former Midland main line travels northwest towards Morecambe, passing the site of the White Lund munitions factory and later the location of the then state-of-the-art coal-fired Lancaster gasworks. The latter opened in 1959, replacing both the town works in Morecambe and the plant in Lancaster, just north of Castle station. The gasworks was the last coal-fired plant to be built in England. The line to Heysham via the Edmondson curve diverges to the left at Torrisholme No. 1 junction - see picture 60.

59. Black 5 no. 44939 is seen passing the site of the Torrisholme (munitions) Factory and, later, the 'new' gasworks on 31st January 1964, working the 2.50pm Heysham Harbour to Stourton (Leeds) freight. In the background, beyond the truck in the sidings, one of the few remaining buildings from the munitions factory can be seen; it appears to be the power station for the shell filling factory that was demolished, despite some opposition, in June 2019. (Ron Herbert)

Torrisholme Junction

60. Ex-LNER B1 no. 61131 *Springbok* hauls a Wakefield-Morecambe excursion on 25th September 1954. It is seen passing the junction, controlled by Torrisholme No. 1 Signal Box. The line diverging to the right is the main line heading to Heysham via the Edmondson Curve.
(CRA Pearsall coll.)

Hest Bank Junction

➔ XIV. This 1933 map shows the busy junction with lines from Bare Lane, Lancaster and Heysham converging towards Morecambe. Hest Bank itself is some miles away, reached via the Morecambe curve east of Bare Lane - see picture 120. The line to Bare Lane is reached out of Euston Road station and from Morecambe Promenade via Hest Bank Junction.

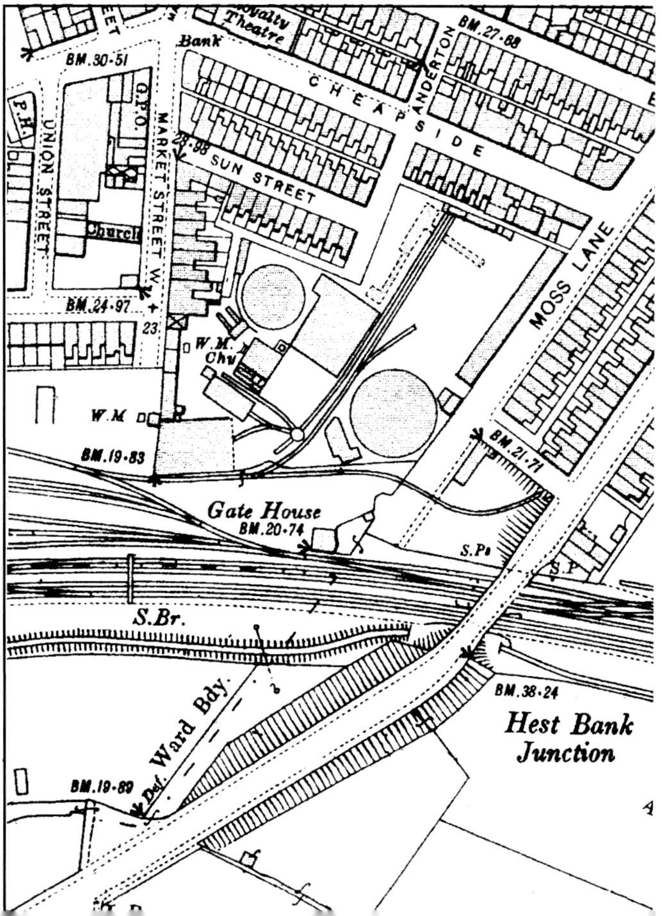

61. A Lancaster-Morecambe service, operated by unit M28220M, passes Hest Bank Junction on 31st July 1960. In the background is Euston Road goods yard; the station beyond and the line to Hest Bank via Bare Lane can be seen at the rear of the train. (Robert Humm coll.)

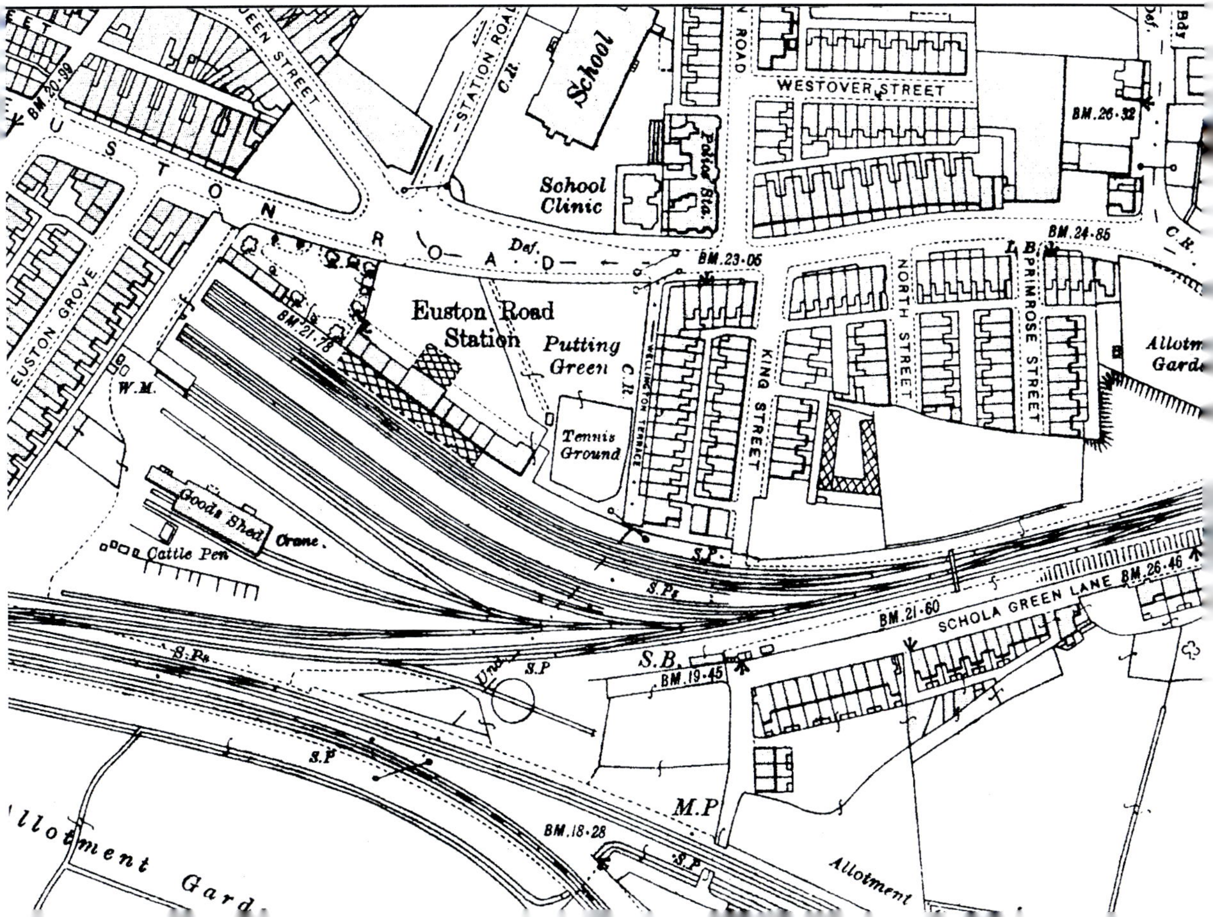

62. BR Standard Class Britannia 7P6F 4-6-2 no. 70013 *Oliver Cromwell* heads the RCTS Lancastrian No. 2 Railtour from Windermere to Morecambe Promenade on 20th April 1968. The train is more or less at the same location as the EMU in the previous picture, but the OLE gantries and wires have gone, Euston Road station and goods are no more and the lines have been rationalised extensively. (Tom Heavyside)

63. Pacer no. 142036 has now left Morecambe and has just passed the signal and ground frame at the much-reduced Hest Bank Junction, and is proceeding to Heysham Port on 7th April 2019. Before doing so, the train would have been held at that point and the driver worked the two-lever ground frame while in communication with Preston Power Box. This shot was taken from the West End Lane/Euston Grove Bridge; in the left foreground is the builder's yard that was once Euston Road goods yard. (Roy Davies)

Town Gas Works

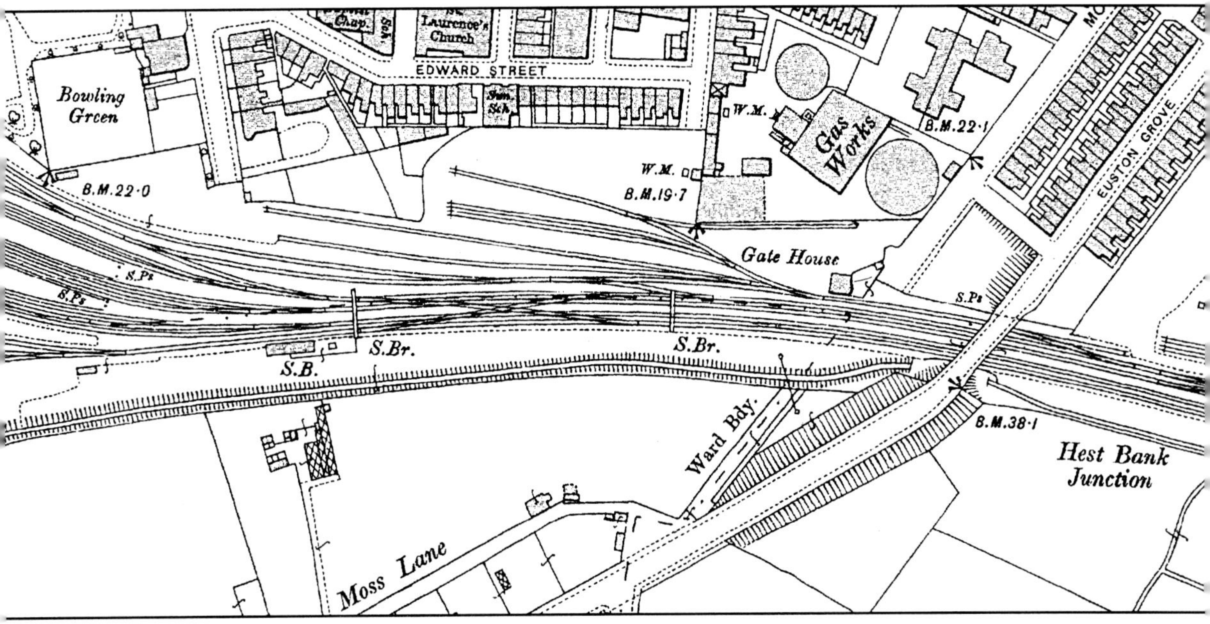

XV. Before reaching Morecambe station, trains passed the rail-served town gasworks and Market Street coal yard, to the left. The site is now occupied by Morecambe Library and the coal yard (closed 1967) by a car park. The Morecambe Gas Company was incorporated in 1857 and the plant came on stream at the close of 1858, but was not rail-connected until just after the council purchased it in 1900. It lasted 100 years before the new gasworks at White Lund replaced both it and the Lancaster plant. The loco that worked the old Morecambe gasworks was *Amy*, ex-T.W.Ward (ship-breakers) in 1930; it was an Avonside 0-4-0ST of 1879 and was scrapped in 1953.

MORECAMBE

64. The original station, a largely timber structure, opened as Poulton-le-Sands on 12th June 1848 and was renamed Morecambe on 1st August 1850 - see Map XVIIa. It was later replaced by a more substantial building, as shown in the next photo. Services operated by LNWR, from Hest Bank via Bare Lane, also used this station but, due to congestion, moved to their own station, Poulton Lane on 1st November 1870. This was later replaced by Morecambe Euston Road in 1886.
(Roy F. Burrows Midland Collection Trust/KRM)

65. An undated photograph shows a well-patronised steam motor train at the rebuilt Morecambe station on the site of the former station completed in 1873. Two driving-trailer cars were converted from this stock to be used in forming the EMUs when the line was electrified. In building terms, the MR station was far grander than its modest predecessor and, while there appears to be no photographic record of the outside of the rebuilt Morecambe station, all is not lost. The frontage was removed substantially and installed at the Promenade station. While the station had a fairly short life, its memory was revived recently by way of a large mural on a house in Edward Street. The excursion line was taken out of use on 16th September 1906 and the station closed shortly thereafter. Steam rail motor coach no. 2234 was converted to an MR officers saloon no. M45010M. (V R Webster collection/KRM)

66. In this circa-1900 photograph at Morecambe, a 2-4-0 locomotive runs tender first on a passenger train consisting of clerestory and arc roofed stock. The station closed in 1907.
(Roy F. Burrows Midland Collection Trust/KRM)

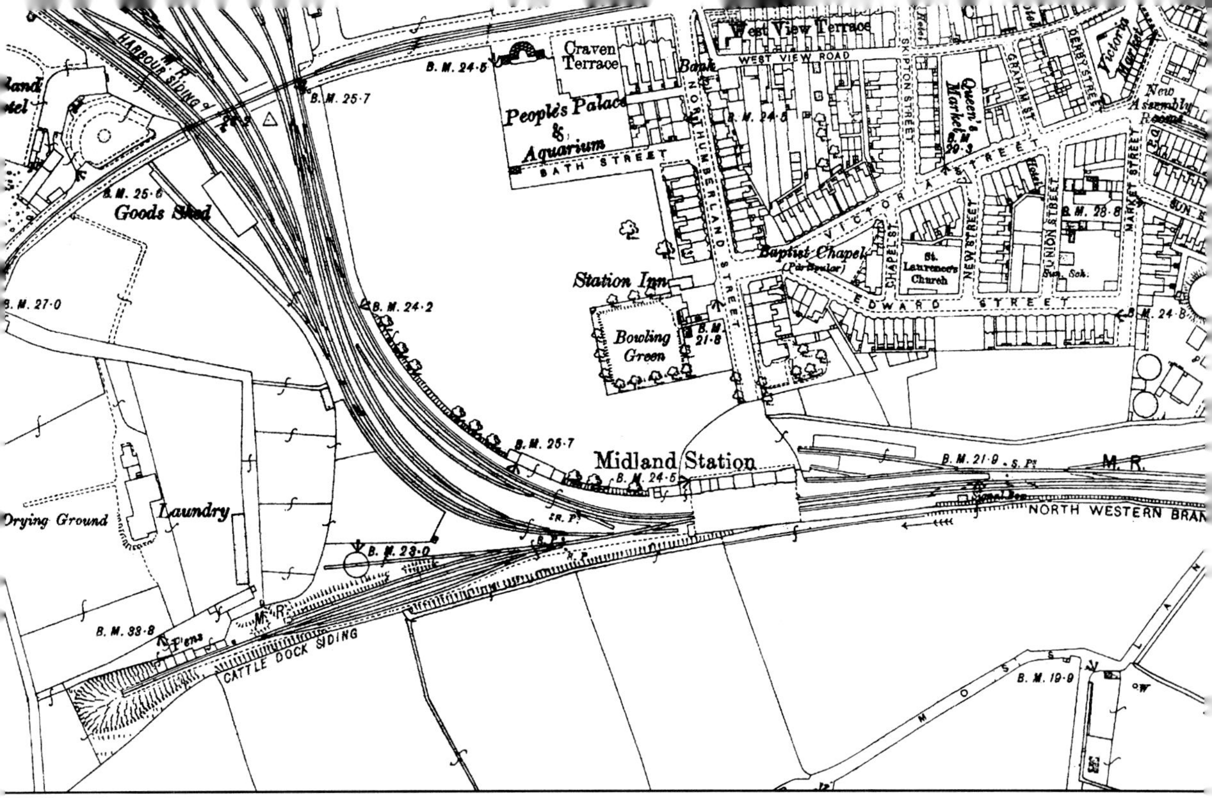

XVI. This map of 1891 shows the Midland station relative to Northumberland Street. The lower lines to the left terminate at the goods facility and cattle dock, while the others led to the harbour and sidings. The current Morecambe station - see picture 112 - is located more or less at the same point. The bowling green is now a car park.

67. In this undated photo, Midland Railway Kirtley 2-2-2 no. 33 is at Morecambe station on what seems to be a one-coach inspection train. This coach has a clerestory roof and open balconies, and appears to be standing at the west end of the station.
(Roy F Burrows Midland Collection Trust/KRM)

MORECAMBE HARBOUR

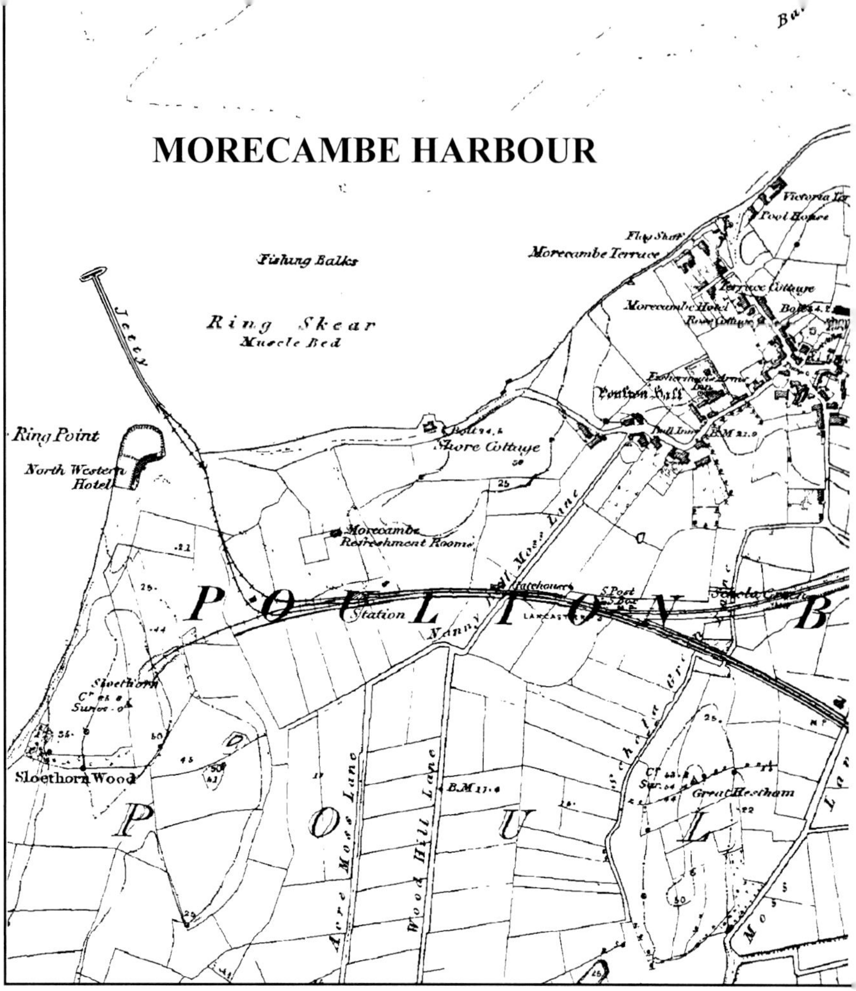

XVIIa. This 1848 6in OS map shows the lines from Lancaster and Hest Bank merging and heading towards Poulton-le-Sands station and a further extension to the wooden jetty on Morecambe Bay. Note the mention of the three hamlets, Poulton, Bare and Torrisholme that later merged to become Morecambe. (*www.old-maps.co.uk*/ Ordnance Survey)

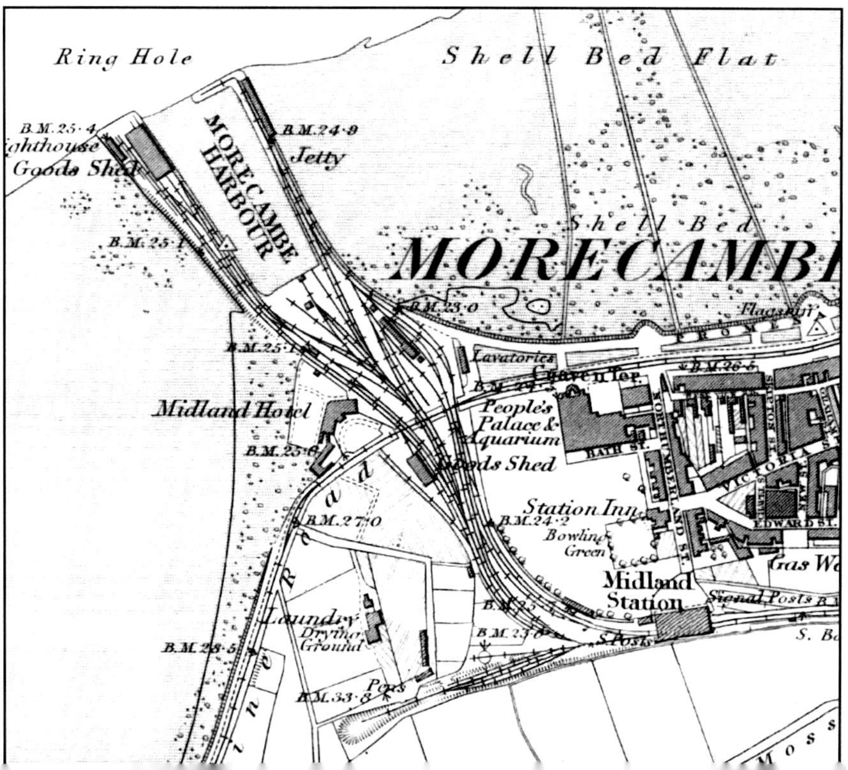

XVIIb. This OS 6in map of 1891 shows the extensive rail network serving both the stone and wooden jetties at the harbour. In the foreground is the original Midland Hotel. Note that this map pre-dates the Heysham branch. The harbour was offered for lease, and Sheffield-based ship-breaker, T.W.Ward moved on site in 1905. The company vacated the site in 1931, much to the delight, no doubt, of the management of the new Midland Hotel that overlooked the jetty.

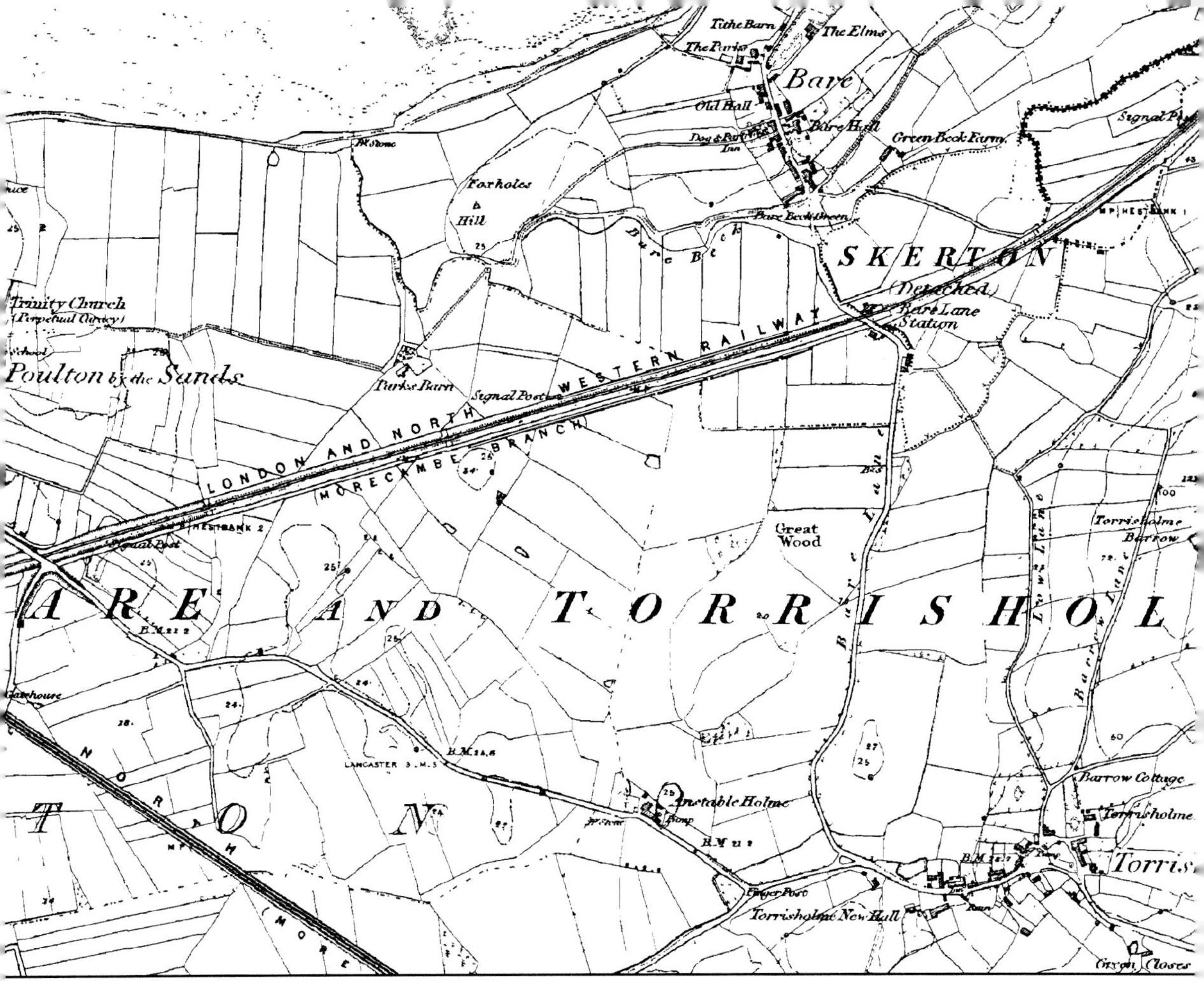

➜ 68. This undated photograph of Morecambe Harbour shows the wooden jetty with the stone jetty behind. The latter was built by the NWR and was completed in 1853 as a wharf and rail terminal for both passengers and goods. (Roy F. Burrows Midland Collection Trust/KRM)

69. This old view of the Harbour station and goods facilities are shown in this period postcard. The full railway layout of the harbour is better illustrated in the 1891 map on the previous pages.
(Roy F. Burrows Midland Collection Trust/KRM)

70. The Harbour station building survives, to this day, as a cafe on the stone jetty. It is deemed a heritage building by the City of Lancaster and bears a plaque referring to its railway and maritime heritage (inset, right). (Roy Davies)

MORECAMBE PROMENADE

71. With the increase in holiday traffic to Morecambe, the station at the end of Northumberland Street had fast become inadequate and, in 1907, the MR built this new terminus a few hundred metres to the west. The station was built re-using walling stone and dressings transferred from the former station. This shot, taken in 1912, shows exclusive use of horse-drawn vehicles of the day, including the MR Express Parcels dray. Note, there is no mention of 'Promenade' in the station name; that was not the railway company style at the time. On 2nd June 1924, the station was renamed Morecambe Promenade by the LMS, to avoid confusion. (J. Alsop coll.)

XVIII. This 1913 map shows the extent of the Promenade station compared with its predecessor; note a line to the harbour sidings was maintained but, by then, the new rail-served port at Heysham was operational. The harbour line disappeared altogether in 1932 when construction of the new Midland Hotel commenced.

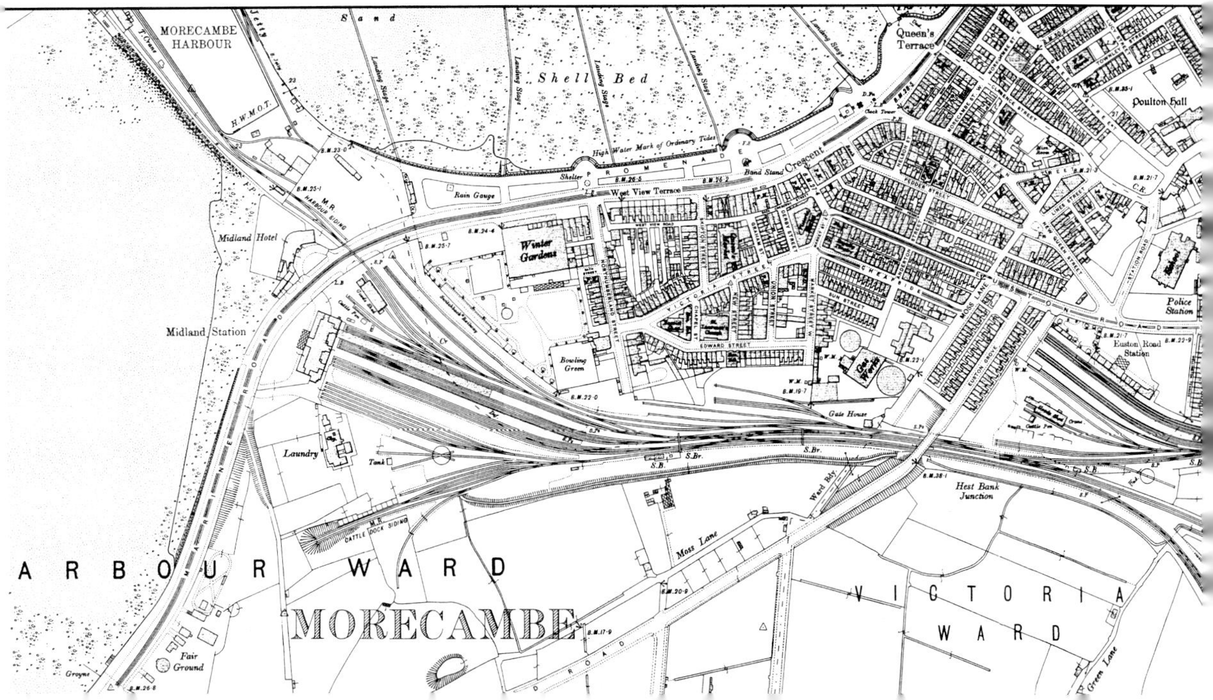

72. An early but undated photo of the main and capacious concourse at Promenade station. In later years the scene was, no doubt, completely transformed on summer Saturdays, when as many as 20 excursions and specials arrived at the resort. (J. Alsop coll.)

73. 'FIRST TRAIN NEW STATION' - it opened officially on 24th March 1907. An MR 2-4-0 heads the first train into the station. That day was a Sunday and would no doubt have accounted for the large crowds on the day. (Midland Railway Study Centre, Derby)

74. This 1933 panoramic view highlights the extent of the Promenade station and the surrounding railway complex. By this time, all connections to the harbour had been severed with the opening of the new Midland Hotel. Beyond the original station site is the town gasworks; this is now occupied by Morecambe Library. Looking beyond the West End Road overbridge, Morecambe Euston Road station and goods yard are to the left behind the gasometer along with the line to Bare Lane, branching off to the left. The MR line to Lancaster continues past the bridge with the Heysham Branch diverging to the right. Under LMS auspices, Promenade would become the town's principal station, but the volume of summer holiday traffic to the resort was such that nearby Euston Road station continued to be heavily used and operated throughout the year, until closure to passengers in September 1962.

The current Morecambe station is located more or less where the signal gantry and box were at the end of Northumberland Street - the row of houses beyond the park on the left. Keen observers will note that it is located more or less on the site of the original town station. The Promenade station building is Grade II-listed so was preserved after railway services were withdrawn, and is known as The Platform, having been transformed into a live entertainment venue and restaurant complex. (Historic England)

MORECAMBE

MIDLAND HOTEL

Telephone : Morecambe 2591

Situated in a superb position on Sea Front.
One minute from the Promenade Station.
Central Heating and every modern comfort.
Good Cuisine. Cocktail Bar.

Enquiries for accommodation will receive the personal attention of the Resident Manager

THE HOTELS EXECUTIVE, BRITISH TRANSPORT, LONDON, N.W.1.

75. In this undated shot, motor coach no. 2236 stands in one of the stabling roads at Morecambe. Three DM cars were built by the MR at its Derby Works and were 60ft in length. Two had Siemens electrical equipment fitted, and Westinghouse equipment was used for the third. The motor coaches were often coupled with one or two driving trailers so could work as one, two or three-car units. On three-car units, the motor coach would usually occupy the centre berth. The three 60ft motor coaches 2236-8 were later numbered 28610 - 28612 by the LMS. (J. Alsop coll.)

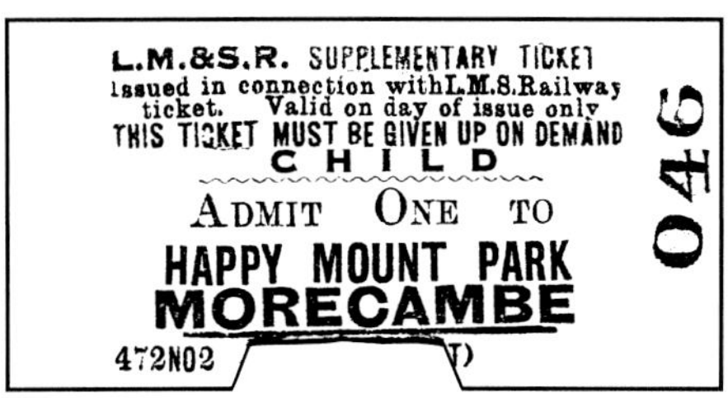

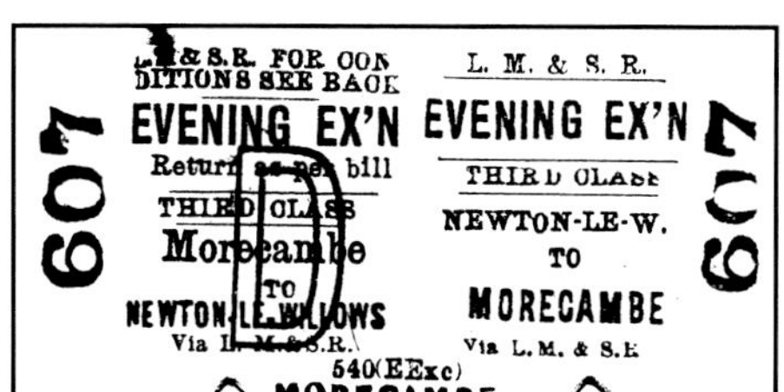

76. Morecambe Promenade signal box and station are pictured on 25th August 1937. The box opened in 1907, replacing an 1892-built signal box located a short distance to the east. On 11th May 1919, a replacement 92-lever Midland Railway tappet frame was installed. While the station had thc suffix 'Promenade' added by the LMS, this doesn't seem to have been the case for the signal box. (Robert Humm coll.)

77. On 2nd February 1951 the EMUs were withdrawn following over 40 years in service, at which point steam loco-hauled stock was used until August 1953. Not long after the steam takeover, Stanier push-pull 2P 0-4-4T no. 41900 stands at Promenade station on 21st May 1951. The locomotives used were numbered 41900 to 41904, having been transferred from the St Albans branch where they had been fitted with vacuum control gear for push-pull work. The wires were re-energised on 17th August 1953. (Robert Humm coll.)

78. Not all visitors to Morecambe came to enjoy the sun, sea and sand. Caledonian Railway loco no. 123 stands at Promenade Station on 18th August 1953. The loco was built in 1886 with works no. 3553 by Neilson & Co at their Hydepark Works in Springburn. It had an unusual wheel arrangement of 4-2-2, but nevertheless won a gold medal at the Edinburgh International Exhibition in the same year. Was it there perhaps to celebrate the re-energising of the lines to Lancaster and Heysham? (CRA Pearsall coll.)

79. EMU no. M28221M stands at Promenade station in this undated photo. Morecambe signal box is just visible. The ex-MR line from Lancaster to Morecambe closed on 4th June 1967, after which the gasworks was at the end of the extended siding from Torrisholme Junction, some 542yds towards Lancaster past the ground frame. The siding closed on 2nd February 1970. (*Colour-Rail.com*)

80. Jubilee no. 45562 *Alberta*, based at Leeds Holbeck, stands at Morecambe heading the 10.35 Summer Saturdays only train to Bradford Forster Square, on 17th June 1967. This train would have run direct to Carnforth, via Bare Lane, over the former LNWR metals. In November 2019, preserved classmate no. 45699 *Galatea* was repainted into British Railways Brunswick green and temporarily renumbered as classmate no. 45562 *Alberta*. (Michael Ellis)

81. Black 5 no. 45025 stands at Morecambe waiting to return to Manchester Victoria with the last steam-hauled Belfast Boat Express on 5th May 1968. No. 45025 was withdrawn from service in August 1968, at the end of steam operations on BR, and is preserved on the Strathspey Railway. (Michael Ellis)

82. In this 5th July 1968 shot, Black 5 no. 45342 is seen leaving Morecambe after reversing with a mixed freight bound for Heysham. With the closure of the former Midland route, all traffic to and from the Heysham line had to reverse at Morecambe. This loco was based at Carnforth 10A and was withdrawn from service about a month later. Note that the train is sporting two brake vans. According to BR London Midland Region rules, dated 1st October 1960: *'Freight trains working into Morecambe Promenade from Euston Road must not exceed 35 wagons and two brake vans, and must have a brake van at each end of the train. On arrival at Morecambe Promenade station, a train proceeding towards Wennington may be made up to a full engine load prior to departure.'* The use of two brake vans avoided the time consumed running around a train, but it became problematical when management decided to dispose of significant numbers of vans; inconvenient perhaps but a a substantial saving on maintenance and repairs. (Tom Heavyside)

Morecambe hotel advertisements, *Bradshaw*, July 1948.

THE REGAL HOTEL

MARINE ROAD EAST, PROMENADE, MORECAMBE

BRITAIN'S BONNIEST BAY
SERVICE—COMFORT—PEACE

Hot and Cold Water in all Bedrooms — Central Heated
Excellent Cuisine — Own Farm Produce
Terms from £7-7-0 per week

Telephones— Hotel 782, Guests 1396
Resident Directors— M. & L. DENISON

A.A. **CONISTON HOTEL** C.V.M.

EAST PROMENADE.

Near Golf Course. Tennis, Bowls, and Open Air Swimming Baths.
Hot & Cold Water in all Bedrooms. Central Heating. Excellent Cuisine.
Ideal Centre for Lakeland Tours. Telephone—737-160
Terms on Application to Resident Proprietors—N. H. FOX and A. YATES
(Late Grand Hotel, Morecambe)

83. Several bogie tank wagons became derailed just outside Promenade station, at a point opposite Morecambe Library, on 31st July 1968. The crane used to re-rail the wagons came from Carnforth and was its final steam-hauled run. (CRA Pearsall coll.)

84. Raildays were not uncommon at Promenade station. Black 5 no. 44932, ex-LMS Ivatt Class 2MT 2-6-0 no. 6441 and a BR diesel Type 4 were seen on 19th and 20th August 1972. The Black 5 is in BR-lined green, the Class 2 in LMS maroon and the Type 4 in BR blue with yellow noses. (Ron Herbert)

85. The named BR Brush Type 4 Class Co-Co 47s allocated to the Western Region were rare visitors to north Lancashire and highly prized by spotters in the 1970s and early 80s. On 31st August 1981 not one but two arrived at Morecambe on day excursions, which was unusual and, more so, because neither had come from the Western Region. No. 47079 *G.J.Churchward*, on the left, is waiting to work the return 1Z21 excursion to Burton on Trent via Crewe; while, on the right, 47077 *North Star*, with the return 1Z32 to Chesterfield, is scheduled to run via Carnforth, Skipton and Leeds. Note the total absence of any OLE steelwork. (Peter Smith)

86. On 4th June 1988, a Birmingham Railway Carriage & Wagon Company-built Class 104 DMU, comprising nos 53494 and 53468, is waiting in platform 1 to form the 18.18 to Lancaster. Given the level of services to Morecambe, Promenade station was much larger than required, although it survived another six years. The stub of the harbour branch and sidings are overgrown, not the best of views for guests at the Midland Hotel with rooms on the land side. (Tom Heavyside)

87. The Granada Telethon Pullman train stands at Morecambe on 19th July 1992, some 18 months before closure of Promenade station. Looking pristine in Regional Railways livery, BR Brush Type 2 diesel A1A-A1A no. 31410 (formerly D5669) toured various northern towns, together with classmate no. 31439, in conjunction with the ITV Charity Telethons, hosted by Michael Aspel. No. 31410 was later named *Granada Telethon*. The carriages were ex-Manchester Pullman stock and now form part of the Statesman set. After going into storage in 2005 at Kirkby Stephen East, it was later moved but suffered irreparable damage at Carnforth and was subsequently scrapped at Booths, Rotherham, in 2014. (Michael Ellis)

88. Morecambe Promenade is in transition. This photograph was taken from the steps of the signal box in the spring of 1994, following closure in February of that year. The refurbished Art Deco Midland Hotel, on the right, is in all its splendour, in stark contrast to the closed station. As mentioned in the caption to photo no. 74, the station building is Grade II listed and the station concourse complex survives as a pub, restaurant and entertainment venue. (David A. Alexander)

3. Down the line to Heysham

Torrisholme Triangle

XIX. This is a map of the 'Torrisholme Triangle' that governed access to Heysham Harbour and surrounding facilities. To the east is the Edmondson curve (Torrisholme Jcn no. 1 to Jcn no. 2) diverging from the main line towards Morecambe (see photo 60) controlled by Torrisholme No. 1 box. From the northwest, the line from Morecambe via Hest Bank Junction turns southwest and the two lines met at the junction controlled by Torrisholme No. 2 box. Both boxes opened on 22nd August 1904. The Edmondson curve and line down to the gasworks was made a siding on 22nd October 1967 in order that coal deliveries to the gasworks could be maintained; the main line was severed some 542yds beyond the White Lund ground frame. The siding closed in January 1970, although the official closure was with effect from 2nd February. See also map XIIIc. Inset pictures: Torrisholme No. 1 box is on the left and Torrisholme No. 2 to the right. (Nigel Mundy)

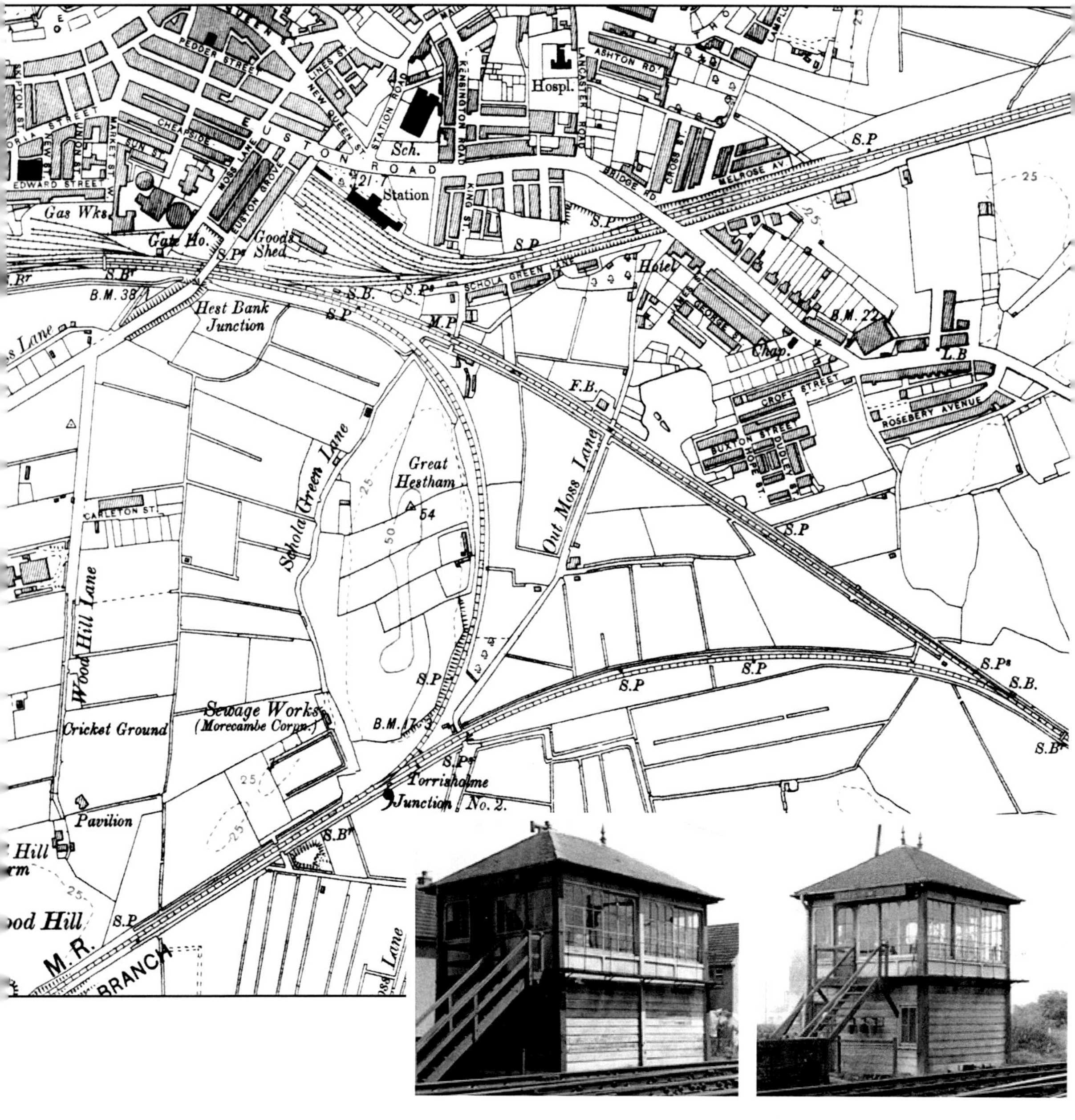

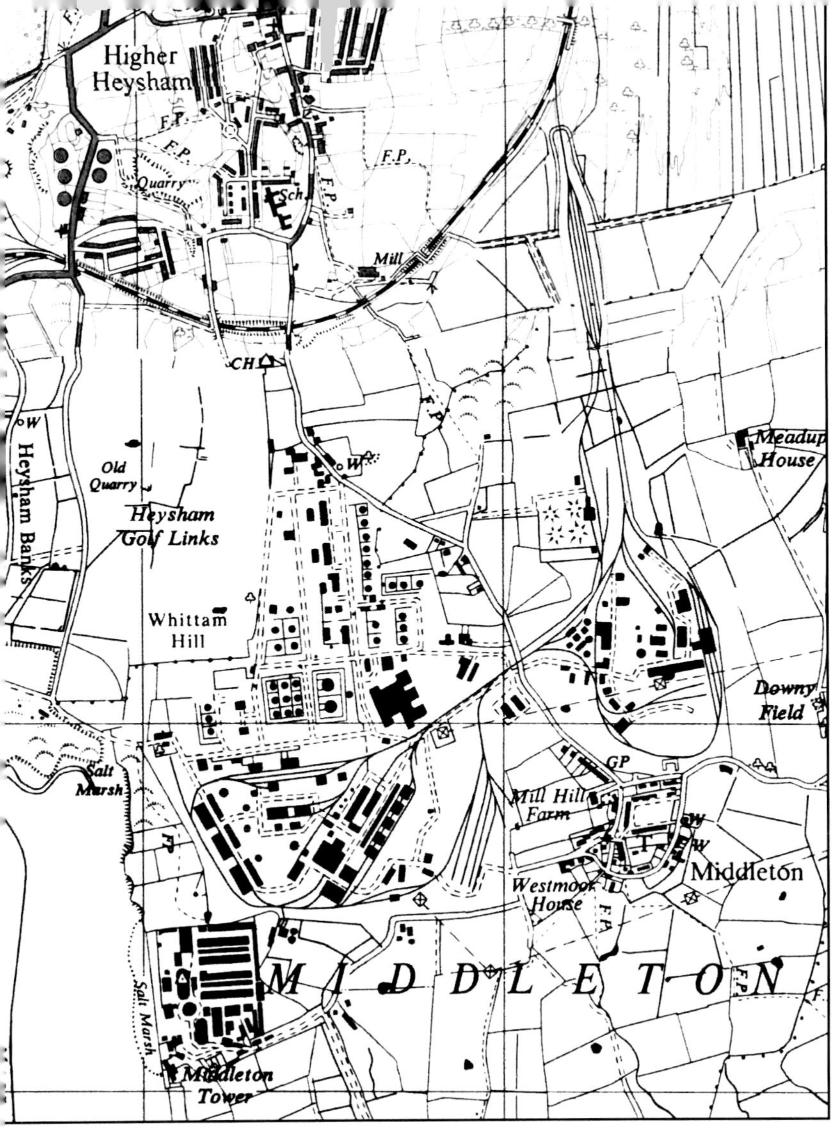

Trimpell Refinery/ Chemical Works

XX. A 1966 1:25,000 map shows the extensive rail network in the Trimpell Refinery. At the top of the network, the line runs into Heysham Moss sidings which, in turn, connects to the Morecambe-Heysham main line - see picture below.

89. In this undated photograph the entrance to Heysham Moss and the refinery complex diverges to the left. A clue to the date is that the up line between Heysham Harbour and Heysham Moss was taken out of use on 30th January 1977; trains would have gained the up line via the crossing, just behind the photographer. In the 1994 rationalisation, the line from Heysham Moss junction to Hest Bank Junction was singled. (Ivan Stewart)

90. This is an undated view of tanks in the loading area within the refinery complex. (ICI)

91. Below is a shot of the fireless locomotive marked ICI Middleton 1964. It is a W. Bagnall 3019 delivered to the refinery in 1952. It was sold in November 1970 to Lakeside Railway Estates Co. Ltd. and put in their museum in the former British Railways motive power depot at Carnforth in September 1976. It was later moved to Shropshire, from where it was sold to a private buyer. It underwent a full cosmetic restoration that was finally completed in May 2010, and now resides in the owner's front garden in deepest Nottinghamshire. (ICI)

➔ 92. On 11th July 1983, BR diesel Type 4 no. 40150 is seen arriving with 7M37 03.40 Haverton Hill-Heysham ammonia train. The extensive sidings were remote from any public roads and difficult to reach by footpath; hence, Heysham Moss sidings were rarely photographed. Note the signal box shown in picture no. 89, at the rear of the train. (Paul Shannon)

➘ 93. Type 4 diesel no. 40073 eases out of Heysham Moss with the Heysham Moss to Haverton service that was booked to run six days a week, Monday to Saturday, and carried anhydrous ammonia from ICI's Billingham plant to its Heysham Moss fertiliser plant. It ran from 5th March 1979 to 22nd April 1986 and shouldn't be confused with a much earlier flow of ammonia in the opposite direction, which ran from 1948 to 1967. Again, note the obligatory guards vans at each end of the train. The signal box was opened 3rd December 1939, serving the sidings that closed in 1986, and closed on 28th April 1987 after an arson attack. (Peter Smith)

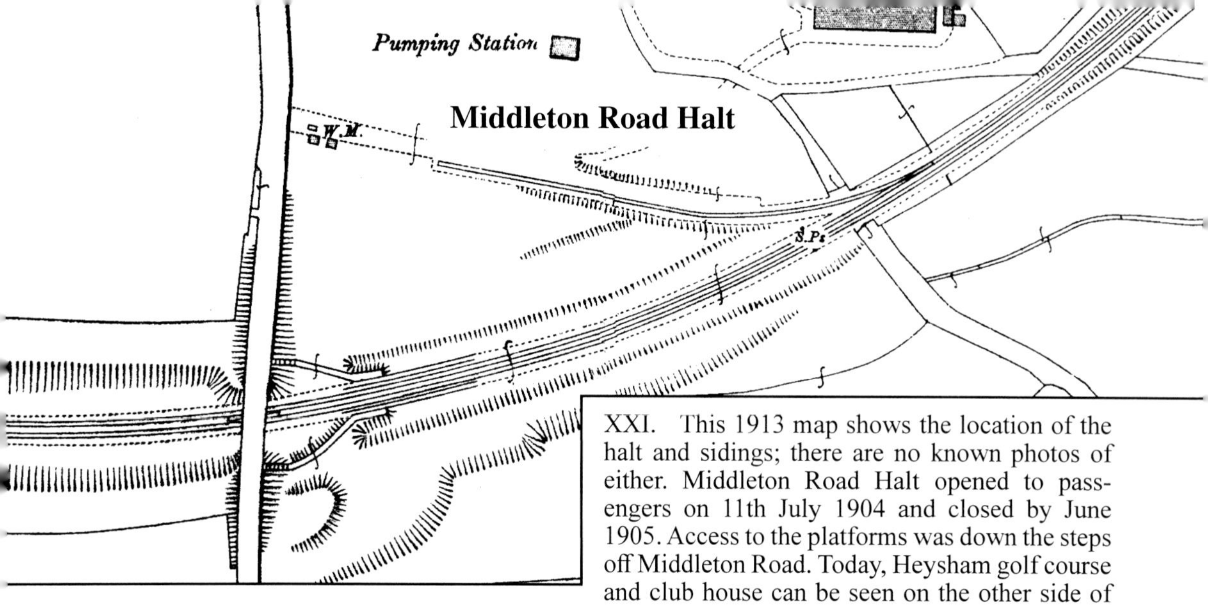

XXI. This 1913 map shows the location of the halt and sidings; there are no known photos of either. Middleton Road Halt opened to passengers on 11th July 1904 and closed by June 1905. Access to the platforms was down the steps off Middleton Road. Today, Heysham golf course and club house can be seen on the other side of Middleton Road, south of the railway line. The siding and ground frame were opened between 1904 and 1910, and closed on 19th July 1965.

Midland Railway Power Station

94. As one approaches Heysham by road or train, this old building comes into view, seen here on 14th December 2013. It was the Midland Railway's generating station at Heysham, built originally for working cranes and other equipment in the docks, but used also to supply the power at 6,600V AC 25 Hz for the Morecambe 'electrics' and is still in use today as a workshop under private ownership. After the lines were re-energised in 1953, trains were powered from the National Grid. (Jan Ford)

Heysham Nuclear Power Station

95. Heysham No. 1 *Lancaster* and Heysham No. 2, behind, were recorded on shed on 5th September 1991. At this time, both were maintained as spare to the two battery locomotives. Note that they were immaculately maintained in the equally pristine loco shed; there were even white cloths laid out on the floor beneath the motion and cylinders to catch any drips of oil. The locos were transferred from Lancaster power station in 1977 and both survive to this day. *Lancaster* is in an unrestored condition at the West Coast Railway Company's Carnforth depot and Heysham No. 2 went into preservation at Southport in 1993 and later moved to Preston in 1999, where it can now be seen cosmetically restored at the Ribble Railway Museum. The same two locos can be seen at Lancaster Power station in picture no. 28. (Gordon Edgar)

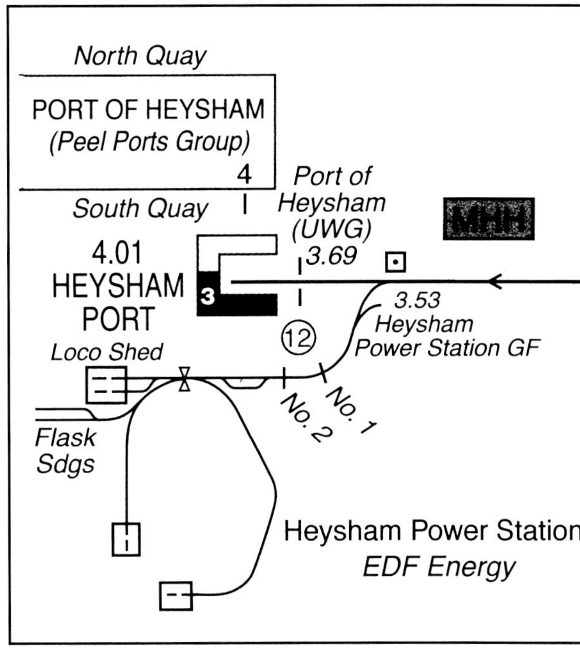

XXII. The rail network within the power station connects to the transfer sidings, where trains to/from Sellafield, operated by Direct Rail Services, terminate. (©TRACKmaps).

96. Later, the power station acquired two electric locomotives. The first was Loco No.1 *Doug Tottman*, built in 1945, which spent much of its working life at Kearsley Power Station near Bolton. In the early 1980s, it was rebuilt and converted to battery operation and transferred to Heysham Power Station for shunting duties around site until 2010. It was then moved into railway preservation at the Electric Railway Museum, Coventry. In 2018, after the museum closed, it was relocated to the Colne Valley Railway in Essex, where it currently resides. The second loco, named *Derek Shepherd*, built in 1936, again spent much of its working life at Kearsley, before moving to Heysham in the early 1980s and being similarly converted. In 2010 it was transferred into railway preservation on the Tanfield Railway in Durham. *Doug Tottman*, on the left, and *Derek Shepherd* were featured in different liveries during their time at Heysham; finally in all over white, sporting the EDF logo. Doug Tottman and Derek Shepherd were senior managers for the CEGB North West Region and both served as station managers at Kearsley Power Station. (EDF)

97. Heysham 1 nuclear power station christened its internal track layout on 16th September 1983. Unfortunately, the station's shunting locos were not ready to receive the dummy flask and wagon to test the handling equipment in the pond hall; so BR was approached to see if a shunting loco could be hired. It was eventually agreed that the Carnforth trip loco, normally a Class 25, could be used. However, on the day, BR Class 40 no. 40024 was assigned to the Carnforth trip. It is seen here nudging the wagons slowly into the pond hall. This was the first and only visit of a BR loco beyond the exchange sidings and on to the internal rail network of the power station. (Peter Smith)

98a. To replace the battery locomotives, the power station acquired a Sentinel diesel locomotive in 2009 built by Rolls-Royce. It is seen here in primer paint on 12th October 2017, about to enter the fuelling hall at Heysham No.1 to collect a spent fuel flask for dispatch to Sellafield later in the day. It was working in this state because the refurbishment had to take place on site in stages, as it needed to be available three days every week to perform its duties around the power station. Later that day, it returned to its shed to have the first coat of new paint applied. (EDF)

98b. Looking resplendent in its dark blue and white livery on shed at Heysham on 9th November 2017, the Sentinel was officially named *Vincent de Rivaz* in honour of the retiring chief executive of EDF Energy plc. (EDF)

↓ 99. Brush Type 2 no. 31200, in Railfreight Grey sporting the 'coal' logo, is seen in the exchange sidings at the power station on 3rd September 1991. This train would have reversed at Morecambe with the loco using the run round loop - see photo 115. Today, flask trains are top and tailed by Direct Rail Services class 68s or 88s, thus obviating the need to run round their charge. (K. Nuttall/*Colour-Rail.com*)

HEYSHAM HARBOUR

100. This 1929 aerial view is of the harbour and railway network at the time. The Harbour station is to the right of the two buildings on the south side of the harbour. Heysham Port was acquired by Mersey Docks and Harbour Company in May 2001, ending any association with railway ownership of the facility. On 22nd September 2005, MDHC was acquired by Peel Ports. In picture no. 43 mention is made of the civil engineers' tip at Heysham; it is at the bottom left of the photo and, together with the land to the right, lies deep under the nuclear power station complex. (Historic England)

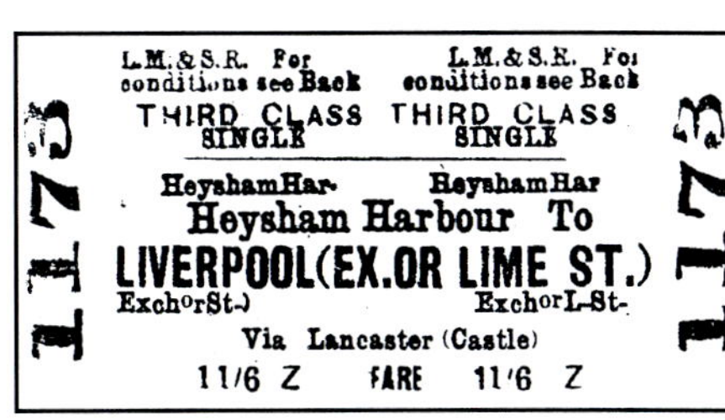

XXIII. This 1933 map, (reduced from its original 25ins to 1 mile scale), reflects more or less what is seen in the previous photograph.

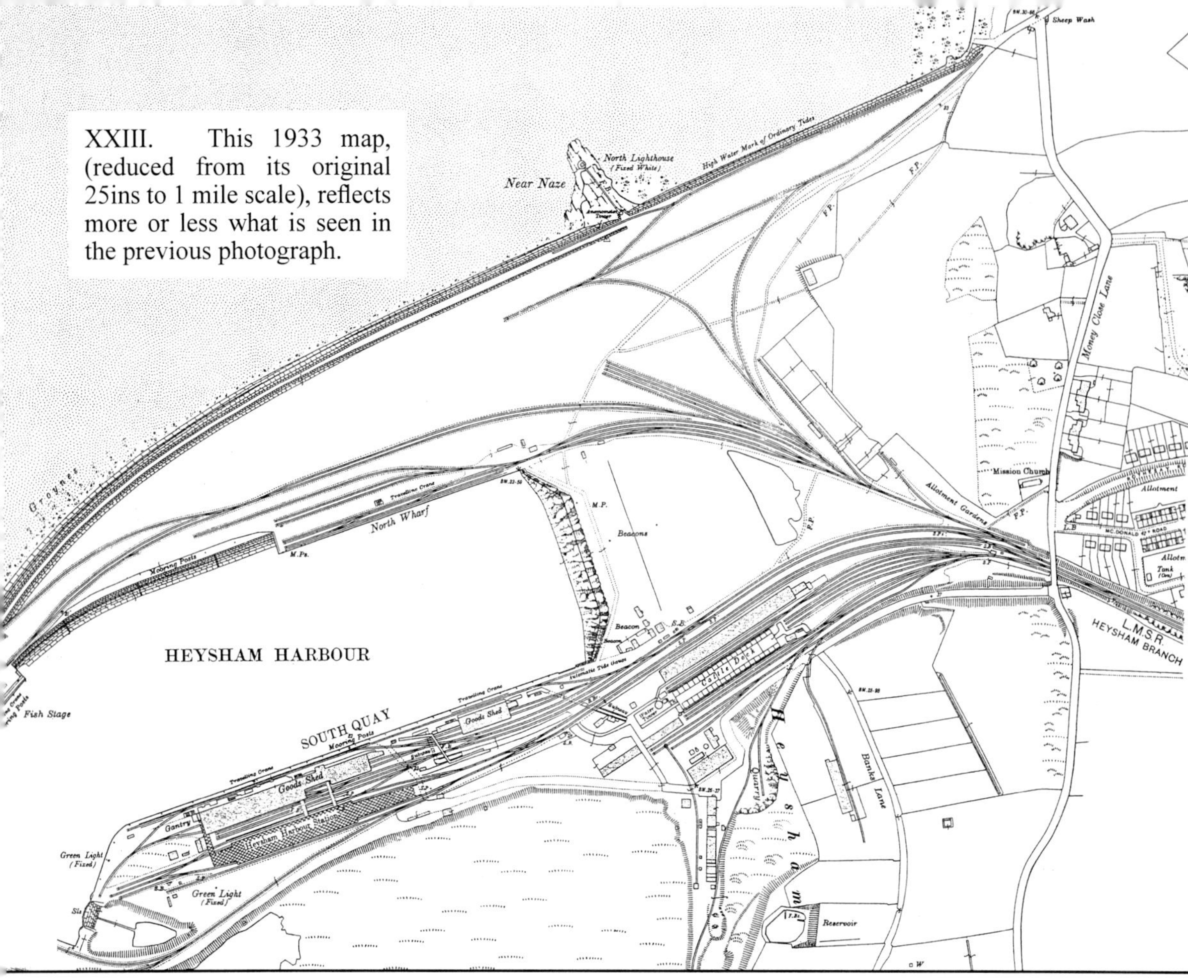

101. A steam motor train stands at platform 1 in this undated photo. The station opened on 11th July 1904 as Heysham Harbour. EMUs were introduced to the line shortly thereafter, but platform 1 was never wired - only platforms 2 and 3, with the latter being used by harbour workers. (J. Alsop coll.)

102. This image of Heysham Harbour station is taken from the cattle bridge, towards the west, on 25th August 1937. Looking at the station, platforms 1, 2 and 3 are seen from left to right. To the left of platform 1 is the line to Heysham tip sidings, where all the spoil and spent ballast was tipped, and, on the horizon to the left of the station buildings, are wagons that would have been used in transporting the waste. The tip is now lost under Heysham power station. (Robert Humm coll.)

103. On 20th August 1965, Set No. 21 is standing at a busy platform 2. (Robert Humm coll.)

104. Black 5 no. 44758 is at Heysham Harbour waiting to depart with the 06.15 'Belfast Boat Express' to Manchester Victoria on 20th April 1968. (ANISTR Keith Widdowson)

HEYSHAM PORT

105. The old station building was demolished and its replacement built on an adjacent site that opened on 4th May 1970 and continued operating until 1975, when sailings to Belfast were withdrawn due to the NI troubles. The station closed to passengers in October of that year, although there was some use of the station during the intervening period. Sailings to Douglas, Isle of Man, resumed and, on 11th May 1987, the austere-looking station was re-opened as 'Heysham Sea Terminal'. Type 4 diesel no. D202 runs round the 10.05 Manchester-Heysham service on 3rd September 1970 at the 'new' Heysham station. On 28th September 1992, the station was again renamed, this time as 'Heysham Port'. Services operated also to and from Blackpool. (CRA Pearsall coll.)

106. On 6th April 2019, Pacer no. 142056 waits to depart Heysham Port with a fairly well-patronised boat train service to Leeds. The Isle of Man ferry, MV *Ben-my-Chree*, can be seen in the background. This train will reverse at Morecambe and again at Lancaster before taking the WCML to Carnforth and on to Leeds via Wennington. In 1994 the layout was rationalised again, as part of the programme of works associated with the building of the current Morecambe station. Canopies were removed and replaced by a single shelter and only platform 3 was retained for boat train services - see map XXII. (Roy Davies)

Heysham Harbour Goods

107. An early view of Heysham Harbour goods sidings was taken in June 1906. (J. Alsop coll.)

108. A busy day in 1968 and much of the layout compares with the previous shot, apart from the addition of the gated fuel sidings. BR Standard Class 4MT Riddles 4-6-0 no.75019 pulls away from the Harbour sidings hauling a mixed freight with brake vans as required by the rules. (D. Preston/*Colour-Rail.com*)

109. This is a view of Heysham Harbour Junction looking west from the old road bridge on 4th August 1970. In the foreground are the piers for the new Rothesay Road bridge that, in decades to come, would link up with the newly-built A683 extension to the M6 motorway, near Halton. The original signal box opened on 4th July 1904 and the new box, to the right, was opened on 3rd May 1970, with closure of the old box on the same day. (CRA Pearsall coll.)

110. It is a wet day at Heysham Harbour, on 29th September 1981, as class 47/3 no. 47367 shunts empty Shell oil tanks, destined for Stanlow, out of the fuel terminal and down the harbour sidings. The 47 had come down from Carlisle Yard, bringing BP oil tanks from Grangemouth but, before they could be stabled in the fuel terminal, the Shell tanks, which had arrived the day before, had to be moved. (Peter Smith)

111. A BR class 108 DMU arrives at Heysham with the 12.04 from Stockport. The signal box was closed on 30th January 1977 and dismantled; it was later donated to the Dean Forest Railway and erected at Lydney Junction. By 1983, oil traffic ceased and the terminal sidings were lifted. With the exception of the siding on the left controlled by the Power Station ground frame, all other sidings were removed and the land given over to HGV parking; in addition the line to Heysham Port station was later singled.
(Tom Heavyside)

➔ An 'England and Ireland via Heysham and Belfast' postcard.
(J.Alsop coll.)

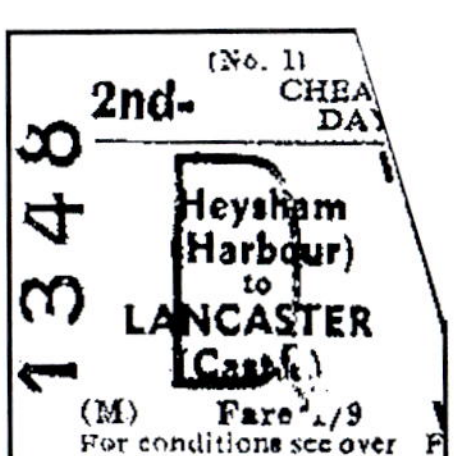

4. Morecambe - Heysham Branch from 1994

MORECAMBE

112. The 1994 station building, taken on 25th September 2020, has a bed of wildflowers outside - the work of the Station Adopters. The current station is built on almost the exact same spot as the original town station, opposite the end of Northumberland Street. Unlike Bare Lane and Heysham Port, that are unmanned, Morecambe has a staffed ticket office open six days a week; both Morecambe and Bare Lane have ticket machines. Under the umbrella of Community Rail Lancashire, and liaising with Network Rail and the train operator, a hierarchy of voluntary groups exists to promote stations and engage with local communities. They are primarily concerned with promoting and lobbying for improved services and facilities along the line; at the sharp end, Station Adopters are the eyes and ears for individual stations, reporting faults and other infrastructure issues and are tasked with implementing various community initiatives such as: tending station gardens and flower beds; involving local schools and creating heritage posters and murals to enhance the traveller's experience and general ambience of stations. Note that the former Promenade station can be seen on the skyline to the right of the lamp post. (David A. Alexander)

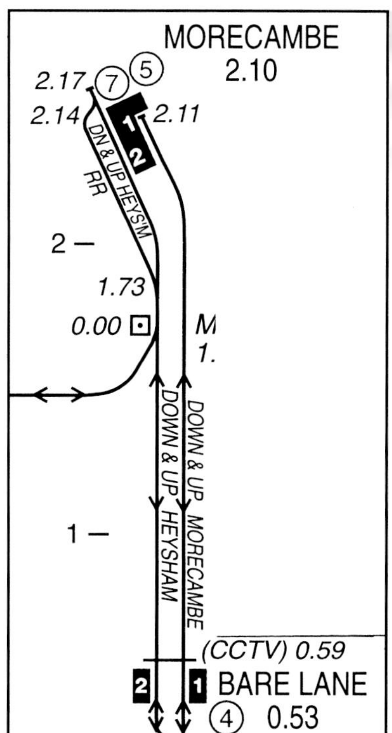

XXIV. This is a schematic of the line from Bare Lane to Morecambe. Since 1994, the two tracks between Bare Lane and Morecambe are operated as two independent single lines with no connection between them beyond Bare Lane. Therefore, only the southern line through platform 2 at the station is connected to the Heysham branch - see picture 116. (©TRACKmaps)

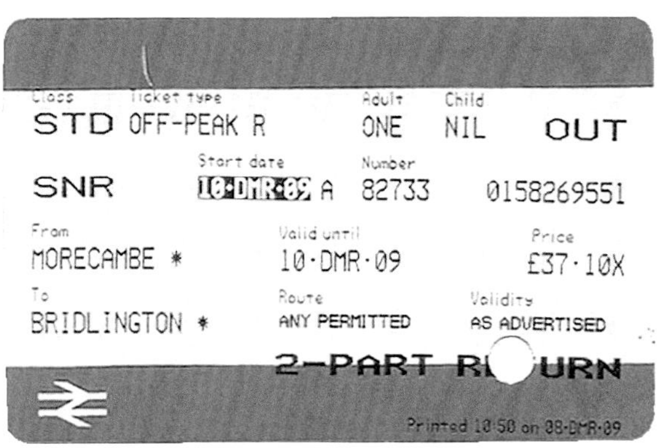

113. Pacer no. 142038 is standing in platform 1 at Morecambe on 5th June 1995 with what will be the 19.45 to Lancaster. That was about a year after the station opened and not much has changed since, other than the addition of a shelter and planters on the platform. (Tom Heavyside)

114. DMU 156460 stands in platform 1 on 6th March 2019 with the early morning service, 05.35 from Lancaster to Windermere via Bare Lane and the Morecambe curve direct to Hest Bank. Until April 2016, the service was operated by TransPennine Express and, prior to the December 2008 timetable change, it ran Windermere–Lancaster–Morecambe–Barrow in the late evening. Since the May 2019 timetable change, this service is now provided by a solitary Monday-Saturday early morning 05.18 train between Lancaster and Morecambe via Carnforth, that uses the Morecambe curve. (Roy Davies)

115. Having just arrived from Lancaster on 7th April 2019, Pacer no. 142036 stands in platform 2 and will reverse and continue as the 13.02 boat train service to Heysham Port, coinciding with the daily sailing to the Isle of Man - see picture 63. The headshunt beyond the train is fitted with spring points set for the run round loop, seen to the left of the DMU. Now that DRS flask trains are top and tailed the loop is no longer used, but would be a useful asset for future excursions to the resort. The start of the footpath and cycleway, that follows the former MR route down to Greyhound Bridge, can be seen on the other side of the railings to the left. It forms part of the western portion of the Way of the Roses that runs from Morecambe to Bridlington (170 miles) and continues on the former Midland route towards Caton. (Roy Davies)

BARE LANE

116. On 2nd April 2021, the flask train comes off the single line and is taking the 'Heysham Branch' through platform 2 at Bare Lane. The flask trains normally run weekly but, surprisingly, it ran on Good Friday. The train is top and tailed by Direct Rail Services nos 68016 *Fearless* and 68006 *Daring*, at the rear. In the background one can see Cottams Farm and beyond is the Lancaster canal. (Michael Ellis)

117. On 1st January 2019, Pacer no. 142045 is seen departing platform 2 at Bare Lane with a Lancaster to Morecambe shuttle. Following withdrawal, the unit was acquired by Kirk Merrington Primary School in County Durham for use as a library. The building in the background is the former station master's house, now in private hands and featured on the BBC TV programme, *Homes Under the Hammer*. (Michael Ellis)

118. Class 158 no. 158755 arrives at Bare Lane with the 08.58 service to Lancaster on 7th July 2020. This shot was taken during the Covid-19 pandemic and the train indicator is not only announcing the next service but also a note: *Face coverings are compulsory*. This, of course, was a requirement on all public transport across the UK during the 2020-21 pandemic. (David A. Alexander)

Mondays to Saturdays

		SO	SX	SX	SO	SX	SO		SO	SX	
Leeds	d	-	-	0819	0819	1218	1218	1418	1726	1726	1918
Shipley		-	-	0832	0832	1233	1233	1433	1740	1740	1932
Bingley		-	-	0837	0837	1237	1237	1438	1745	1745	1937
Keighley		-	-	0842	0842	1243	1243	1443	1752	1752	1943
Skipton	a	-	-	0855	0855	1256	1256	1457	1807	1808	1957
Skipton	d	0519	0522	0856	0856	1258	1258	1458	1808	1810	2000
Gargrave		0525	0528	0902	0902	1304	1304	1504	1814	1815	2006
Hellifield		0534	0537	0910	0910	1312	1312	1513	1822	1824	2014
Long Preston		0537	0540	0913	0913	1315	1315	1515	1825	1826	2017
Giggleswick		0545	0548	0921	0921	1323	1323	1523	1833	1834	2025
Clapham		0554	0556	0929	0929	1331	1331	1531	1841	1843	2034
Bentham		0601	0603	0935	0935	1337	1337	1538	1848	1849	2040
Wennington		0606	0608	0940	0940	1343	1343	1543	1853	1855	2046
Carnforth	a	0620	0622	0956	0956	1359	1359	1559	1909	1911	2102
Lancaster	a	0632	0631	1006	1006	1409	1410	1608	1919	1924	2115
Bare Lane	a	-	-	1022	1024	1419	1420	1628	1940	1947	-
Morecambe	a	-	-	1027	1028	1423	1424	1633	1945	1951	-

Sundays

Leeds	d	0831	1033	1329	1532	1730	-	-	-		
Shipley		0845	1046	1342	1545	1743	-	-	-		
Bingley		0852	1050	1346	1549	1747	-	-	-		
Keighley		0859	1056	1352	1555	1753	-	-	-		
Skipton	a	0915	1108	1404	1608	1806	-	-	-		
Skipton	d	0917	1110	1406	1609	1809	-	-	-		
Gargrave		0922	1115	1412	1615	1815	-	-	-		
Hellifield		0931	1124	1420	1623	1823	-	-	-		
Long Preston		0934	1126	1423	1626	1826	-	-	-		
Giggleswick		0941	1134	1431	1634	1834	-	-	-		
Clapham		0949	1142	1439	1642	1842	-	-	-	-	-
Bentham		0956	1148	1445	1648	1848	-	-	-	-	-
Wennington		1001	1153	1450	1653	1853	-	-	-	-	-
Carnforth	a	1015	1209	1506	1709	1909					
Lancaster	a	1027	1219	1518	1721	1921					
Bare Lane	a	1035	1236	1529	1730	1934					
Morecambe	a	1039	1240	1533	1734	1938					
Heysham Port	a	-	1259	-	-	-					

Notes
SO Saturdays only.
SX Mondays to Fridays only.

Northern Train timetable, May 2021.

LANCASTER

119. Pacer no. 142041 is setting off from platform 2 at Lancaster, bound for Morecambe, with the 17.12 on 30th April 2019. After leaving Lancaster, this train will cross the Carlisle Bridge (photo 53) and leave the WCML via the Morecambe South Junction heading towards Bare Lane. (Roy Davies)

HEST BANK

120. The trunk route between London and Glasgow is always referred to as the WCML, but Morecambe Bay is the only point along the whole route where it actually runs near the West Coast. Here, Pacer no. 144002 is about to join the WCML at Hest Bank, at the site of the former station, with the 15.36 Morecambe to Leeds on 3rd March 2019; this is one of the three Sunday afternoon services, at the time, that went direct from Morecambe to Carnforth via the Morecambe curve. This train will continue to Leeds via Carnforth and Wennington. (Roy Davies)